RELIGION AND
SOVIET FOREIGN POLICY
1945–1970

The Royal Institute of International Affairs is an unofficial body which promotes the scientific study of international questions and does not express opinions of its own. The opinions expressed in this publication are the responsibility of the author.

The Institute gratefully acknowledges the comments and suggestions of the following who read the manuscript on behalf of the Research Committee: Michael Bourdeaux, Raymond Hutchings, and Roger Morgan.

Religion and Soviet Foreign Policy 1945-1970

WILLIAM C. FLETCHER

Published for

THE ROYAL INSTITUTE OF
INTERNATIONAL AFFAIRS

by

OXFORD UNIVERSITY PRESS
LONDON

1973

Oxford University Press, Ely House, London W.1

GLASGOW NEW YORK TORONTO MELBOURNE WELLINGTON
CAPE TOWN IBADAN NAIROBI DAR ES SALAAM LUSAKA ADDIS ABABA
DELHI BOMBAY CALCUTTA MADRAS KARACHI LAHORE DACCA
KUALA LUMPUR SINGAPORE HONG KONG TOKYO

ISBN 0 19 214993 8

PRINTED IN GREAT BRITAIN BY
THE EASTERN PRESS LIMITED, LONDON AND READING

To a pleasant ally

Contents

Preface

The study which follows is an attempt to survey a complex and almost entirely neglected aspect of Soviet foreign policy. In a number of conversations with James Fawcett, Director of Studies of the Royal Institute of International Affairs, and others on the Chatham House staff, it became apparent that the student of international relations has no readily available access to the contribution which Soviet citizens engaged in religious activities make to the relations of the USSR with other countries and organizations in the international domain. A consensus quickly developed that this subject warrants attention, for without some awareness of the comparatively vigorous engagement of Russian religious figures in international life the student of contemporary foreign affairs is inadequately equipped for evaluation of the total range of his subject. This book, then, was undertaken as a modest initial attempt to meet the need.

It should be emphasized, of course, that the present study does not necessarily represent the views of any of the people with whom I have discussed these matters over the years. Quite candidly, any accurate insights which it contains are primarily, if not exclusively, the result of their kindness in sharing their experience with me. So I cannot lay claim to them for myself; but I can (and willingly do) file a claim for exclusive right to any mistaken judgements or distorted evaluations which may have crept into the text. These are my responsibility alone and are in no measure attributable to those with whom I have conferred.

I owe a special debt of gratitude to the support of Chatham House in the preparation of this study. The Institute very kindly gave me a grant which allowed a period of work abroad on some of the Far Eastern aspects of the subject.

The individuals to whom I owe a debt of gratitude are many. My former colleagues Bernhard Wilhelm and Silvia Stöcker merit my profound gratitude, which I am delighted to express here. Rena Fenteman of Chatham House devoted a great deal of energy and contributed no little insight during the preparation of the study. Sarah Hearn and Vicki

Monnard gave indispensable assistance in manuscript preparation. Finally, in this as in all other studies I have undertaken, my wife by her patience and support made a contribution which is enormous.

W. C. F.

Lawrence, Kansas
1 May 1972

Abbreviations

ACPA	All Christian Peace Assembly
BWA	Baptist World Alliance
CCIA	Commission of the Churches on International Affairs
CPC	Christian Peace Conference
CSR	Československá Socialistická Republika
EPS	*Ecumenical Press Service*
RCDA	*Religion in Communist Dominated Areas*
ROEC	Russian Orthodox Eastern Church
WCC	World Council of Churches
WFB	World Fellowship of Buddhists
WFB Bulletin	*World Fellowship of Buddhists News Bulletin*
ZhMP	*Zhurnal Moskovskoi Patriarkhii*

1 Introduction

SOVIET foreign policy has emerged in the past quarter century as one of the major determinants of contemporary history. That corner of the world where life is not influenced in some measure by the international interests and activities of the USSR is very remote indeed, for throughout the community of nations public—and often private—life is subject to the impact of Soviet foreign relations in manifold ways. The Soviet Union and its international interests loom large in the confrontation between East and West which has been the prime factor in much of the political history of the post-war world. Accordingly, Soviet foreign policy has been the subject of intensive study on a massive scale in the West, and rightly so, for to understand international life and to act intelligently and effectively therein is inconceivable without detailed knowledge of this major determinant of world affairs. This study will survey an aspect of Soviet foreign policy which has hitherto been largely neglected—the role played by religion, or, more exactly, the role of religious organizations and individuals in Soviet foreign affairs.

It must be emphasized that religion represents but one of a multitude of avenues to the implementation of Soviet aspirations in the international arena, and a subsidiary one at that, always ancillary, and sometimes very peripheral, to the major efforts of Soviet foreign policy. Religion is a minor aspect of the vast array of factors which enter into a successful foreign policy in the modern world; to neglect it entirely would demonstrate an incomplete appreciation of the subject, but to assign to religion an unwarranted degree of importance would be no less detrimental to a balanced appraisal.

Soviet foreign policy may be summarized under a number of major headings. Most obvious are the normal, traditional channels of international diplomacy. The USSR maintains a large, experienced corps of foreign service officers, and its diplomatic missions in the seemingly innumerable countries of the contemporary world are well supported, competently staffed, and impressively equipped. In addition, Soviet diplomacy is well buttressed with support operations. Soviet foreign trade is of some importance in the international economy. The foreign aid programme of the USSR has been expanding rapidly since the 1950s, serving as a major factor in the nation's relations with many

1

countries. Soviet military power is of immense influence in international life—directly, as in recent relations with Czechoslovakia, indirectly in military and arms aid, as in the Middle East, Vietnam, and elsewhere, or negatively as a powerful potential determinant of the limits of action which other countries may conduct with impunity, as in the Sino-Soviet conflict.

A second major channel for Soviet influence in international affairs is to be found in the category of indirect relations, beyond the normal boundaries of trade, aid, and diplomacy. The fraternal and co-operative relationships with national and local Communist parties throughout the world (although their affiliation with the Communist Party of the Soviet Union is by no means uniform) are undoubtedly an asset to Soviet foreign policy in many areas of the world. In addition, the USSR maintains a highly developed apparatus for international espionage and intelligence activities, which has enjoyed spectacular success. The Soviet posture in international affairs has been immensely strengthened by the hard work and careful, successful planning of specialists in these activities, whether in facilitating the acquisition of technical processes, as in the development of atomic capabilities, or in providing advanced, detailed knowledge of military or diplomatic intentions, as during World War II. Somewhat more amorphous is the considerable number of non-Communist dissident organizations in many countries, which, in their deep dissatisfaction and distress with the prevailing political or social system, have served, wittingly or unwittingly, as temporary adjuncts to Soviet ambitions in their area, and have in a number of cases been the recipients of large-scale financial and other support from the USSR.

A third important aspect of Soviet foreign policy is the contribution which can be made by public opinion throughout the world. The USSR was the pioneer in the development of the concepts, methods, and techniques of modern propaganda, and the resources and facilities devoted to Soviet propaganda for the international audience, currently and over the past half century, are probably without precedent. Particularly since the mid-1950s much effort has gone into the image-building process, with the development and use of a vast array of non-propaganda activities designed to elicit a favourable reaction to the USSR, whether generally or in specific matters. The waning of the cold war is merely the most obvious illustration of the degree of success which the USSR has enjoyed in overcoming the negative attitude towards Stalin's Russia which formerly was widespread.

The institutional bases of Soviet foreign policy are numerous. First there is the Ministry of Foreign Affairs with its many diplomatic establishments—embassies, consulates, missions, etc. Amtorg and Comecon are but two of the institutions of Soviet trade. The military organizations of the USSR are augmented by such international structures as the Warsaw Alliance. Communist Party institutions exist throughout the world. The KGB (Committee of State Security, responsible for nonmilitary intelligence activities) and the GRU (State Intelligence Directorate, for military intelligence) are simply the most prominent of a wide variety of institutional structures in the field. TASS (the Soviet news agency) is but the most prominent of many organizations devoted to propaganda, and the various institutional programmes for international exchange (in industry, education, scholarship, the arts, and so on) form only a part of the structured capabilities for the image-building process. And in all these organizations, the Communist Party is by law, and usually in fact, the directing authority.

Thus the religious institutions which participate in Soviet international affairs—the Christian Churches (Russian Orthodox, Russian Baptists, Baltic Lutherans, etc.) and the institutions of Islam and Buddhism in the USSR—form only a small component of the variegated, highly developed structures of Soviet foreign affairs. The religious institutions are unique, however, in their fundamental basis. Unlike the secular institutions enumerated above, and all other institutions of Soviet society, the religious organizations do not, ultimately, look to the Communist Party as the foundation of their existence and as the final arbiter of their aspirations and policies, but to something else. In the course of this study it may appear that at times this institutional difference has had little practical effect in foreign relations, but the fact that the religious organizations are essentially non-Party (or, according to Soviet ideological interpretation, anti-Party) institutions ensures that their role in international affairs is unique in certain respects, and hence religion must receive special, detailed attention in the study of Soviet international relations.

Religion's primary role in Soviet foreign policy is in the third of the above categories, in the field of public opinion. It is true that few of the other aspects have not at one time or another benefited from a religious contribution. Religious participation in diplomatic receptions within the USSR has been reciprocated by diplomatic representation at religious functions in foreign countries. Infrequently, religious institutions have made a contribution to foreign aid (for charitable purposes).

From time to time, military ventures have received the energetic, if verbal, support of religion. On at least one occasion, religious co-operation with Soviet foreign intelligence has been documented. Non-Communist or quasi-Communist organizations acting in harmony with Soviet foreign policy on numerous occasions have enjoyed the vigorous support of religious organizations in the USSR.[1] However, the great majority of the services which have been rendered by institutional religion have come in the field of image-building and propaganda. Even here, religious institutions make only a minor, fractional contribution to the total Soviet effort; hence to maintain a proper perspective it must continually be borne in mind that religion is by no means a dominant or major factor in Soviet foreign policy.

This study will make no attempt to evaluate the significance of the religious component in Soviet foreign policy in percentile or proportional terms. Such an evaluation would entail a perilous excursion into the non-verifiable, for so complex is the content of international relations that an attempt to analyse the quantitative impact of any single aspect of a particular venture renders subjective evaluation nearly inevitable. Depending on one's ideological and philosophical presuppositions and one's particular approach to *realpolitik*, religion's importance can be assessed in minimal or in the most grandiose terms. Demonstrably, religion has been an effective adjunct to Soviet foreign policy, and this work will confine itself to an attempt to delineate the ways in which these adjunctive services have been rendered, without indulging in experiments in quantitative evaluation.

Soviet foreign policy is manifestly a complex subject; thus to keep the treatment manageable it has been necessary to operate within certain limits. No attempt will be made to survey or analyse Soviet policies except as they are relevant to the religious dimension. An acquaintance with international affairs, and especially with events since the mid-1950s, will be assumed. Even where international relations of some complexity impinge on the role of religious contributors to Soviet foreign policy, only minimal analysis will be attempted. This study will endeavour to maintain a focus, forgoing any attempt to give a full, rounded, general picture of Soviet foreign policy in the hope that a comprehensible understanding of the specific role of religion will emerge.

Religion's part in Soviet foreign policy has evolved out of the peculiar combination of circumstances which have defined Church-State relations in the USSR since World War II. That there can be any symphony of action between the Russian Church and the Soviet State is an ideological anomaly, for Marxism-Leninism contains a deep stream of adamant hostility to all religion. The dogma of the incompatibility of religion with a Communist—or even, ideally, a Socialist—society is far from a dead letter, and the Communist Party remains firmly committed to atheism. At no time has the Soviet State modified its conviction that religion eventually must disappear completely from human society, and energetic measures of intensive pressure have been, and continue to be, applied to accomplish that goal. It is precisely these antireligious policies, effectively executed, which have led to the present incongruous partnership of Church and State in foreign affairs.

The first ten years of Soviet rule in Russia convinced the leadership of the Russian Orthodox Church that hostility towards the new regime, or even political neutrality, provided the Church with no means of defence against the power of the hostile State.[2] In 1927 the head of the Church, Metropolitan Sergii, convinced that the State had ample means for the destruction of the institutional Church (i.e. as an organized, corporate body functioning within Soviet society) reversed the Church's position and offered to the State the full support of the Church in all political matters, in the hope that the State would reciprocate by withholding its power to liquidate the Church. The State was little interested in this offer, and the next twelve years were to demonstrate that its power to effect the physical destruction of the institutional Church was far from imaginary. The intensive campaign against religion which began in 1929 and continued largely unabated for the next decade wreaked havoc on institutional religion in the USSR. By 1939 the Russian Orthodox Church was on the brink of complete dissolution, and as an institution in society it had virtually disappeared. It was only the coming of World War II which halted the process, for the State belatedly discovered it had need of the Church (or any other group, for that matter, which might offer support in the crisis of war). A bargain was struck with the Church, and it is this bargain which has provided the basis for all subsequent religious activity in international affairs.

Essentially, the State granted certain minimal concessions to the Church, marginally sufficient to ensure its continued survival in the country, in return for the Church's unwavering support in political activities, primarily on the international scene. From the State's point of view, the advantages which may accrue from the political co-operation of the Church were deemed sufficient to outweigh the ideological annoyance of a delay in the eventual disappearance of organized religion from Soviet society. From the Church's point of view, the advantages of continued institutional existence in Soviet society were deemed sufficient to outweigh the religious—and sometimes ethical— incongruity of subservience to an antireligious State in political matters. This unwritten concordat between Church and State is to be discerned in the background of every activity of the Church in international politics. The Church is often able to find a genuine confluence of goals in serving its society in this way, especially where the State expresses a commitment to social justice, peace, and other humanitarian ideals; but if the Russian Church at times may seem somewhat less agitated by questionable or unjustifiable activities on the part of its government than might be the norm for Churches in different circumstances, it should be borne in mind that the terms of the bargain stipulate that such political services, even if sometimes distasteful, are the means of ensuring the Church's continued survival as an institution in Soviet society. Alternative means of securing that goal have yet to be suggested.

For their part, those Western Churches which have interacted with Soviet churchmen in international life are motivated by a number of considerations which encourage such ventures. Perhaps the initial motivation is not dissimilar to a natural curiosity, for at first glance the Russian approach to the faith is exotic indeed. Such curiosity has sound theological support, for the peculiar historical experience of the Russian Church, which for almost a millennium practised Christianity with little or no contact with the West, surely can be expected to have yielded unique insight into the common faith. The ecumenical movement itself is premised in no small degree on a desire to gain a deeper appreciation of the profundities of the religion through mutual interchange of experiences and exposure to the different traditions of the Christian faith. Allied with this emphasis in the ecumenical movement is an aspiration to achieve effective Christian unity despite political obstacles which may intervene. In many respects this attitude is the religious expression, if not the epitome, of that broader sentiment for building bridges across political barriers, of actively seeking ways of healing the dangerous and debilitating malaise of political hostility in the human family. Finally, many Western Christians display a degree of scepticism towards shibboleths which the more outspoken foes of Soviet international activities have been repeating for the past twenty-five years and more.

This study will not attempt to examine in detail the motivations and aspirations of those individuals and Churches which have been prominently engaged in these activities, but will endeavour to adhere rather strictly to a delineation of those areas in which religion has been relevant to Soviet foreign policy interests. To the degree possible, the treatment will be restricted to description, rather than analysis. Certainly the temptation to embark on excursions into theological or philosophical speculation will be resisted. Many of the aspects which enter into the total picture from points of view other than that of Soviet policy will be treated sparingly, if at all. All these activities have theological and philosophical overtones; these will be elucidated only to the degree necessary for an understanding of religion's role in Soviet foreign policy. Ecumenical goals and activities will not be examined in areas which are not of direct relevance to the immediate issues of this study. Considerations of Church politics, of the dynamics of an effective and harmonious interrelation between religious organizations, will not be mentioned except as they become intertwined with Soviet foreign policy considerations.

Similar limitations will be accepted regarding the converse consideration, which is the ideology, traditional heritage, and operational habits of secular Soviet policy. To the extent that Churches co-operate with Soviet foreign policy, they must adapt themselves in some measure to its prevailing practices; hence a complete understanding of any particular action of joint interest to Church and State presumes a degree of knowledge of these prior aspects. The ideological structure of Soviet international activities will not be treated in depth, lest the study reach unmanageable proportions. In particular, no attempt will be made to treat Communism as a religion, despite the admitted fact that it bears many of the attributes of a religion: a demand for absolute devotion, an inevitable and pre-ordained destiny for human affairs, a body of sacrosanct writ and cherished dogma, infallible interpretations, charismatic leaders—the list can be amplified indefinitely. This study will maintain the distinction between ideology and religion, and will concentrate only on the latter.

A further limitation which may not be quite so obvious will appear in the course of this work. The treatment will concentrate on the role which religion has played in furthering Soviet foreign policy designs; little or no attention will be given to the converse, which is the possible or actual inverse effect of such activities, in which religion induces Soviet policy to alter its programmes. To date, little or no evidence has become available which would delineate specific instances of changes of plan induced by religious participants in Soviet foreign affairs—with the possible exception of one recorded instance in which a proposed

MVD operation was modified slightly as a result of Metropolitan Nikolai's co-operation in the mid-fifties.[3] This is not to deny the possibility that Russian churchmen may have been able to exert an influence on the political activities to which they have offered their support; such possibilities, however, must remain conjectural in the absence of data.

Foreign policy considerations do, of course, have an impact on the determination of domestic religious policies. This is implicit in the bargain described above. A more striking example is to be found in the treatment of the Jewish minority in the Soviet Union. Time and again Soviet Jews have come under severe attack in the wake of events on the international plane. The increased anti-Semitism in the USSR since 1967 seems directly connected with relations with the Arab world following the Six-Day War of 1967, and the repeated campaigns against 'international Zionism' have on numerous occasions threatened to spread over into general anti-Semitism directed against all Jews regardless of their own attitudes towards such international dimensions of the faith. The Jewish community in the USSR has not been permitted the facilities of a central organization, and has had very few opportunities indeed for joint action with the State in foreign affairs. As a result, Jews have profited little from the unwritten concordat with religion which has characterized the post-war period, and their domestic life is continually affected by considerations of Soviet international affairs.

Because this study deals with Soviet foreign policy, few occasions will arise for examination of the domestic repercussions of religion's international role. It should be noted, however, that such effects are pronounced, and, indeed, for many of the events and activities to be discussed, there will be a corresponding effect in the domestic circumstances of religion.

Every attempt will be made to minimize and, where possible, suppress altogether any tendency to append value judgements to the treatment of the events and endeavours of the religious contribution to Soviet foreign policy. It would be disingenuous to claim that a subject of this nature can be approached without preconceptions and preferences, and it would be unrealistic to assume that such disabilities can be prevented from influencing the treatment, even if unconsciously, at one point or another. However, it is the purpose of this study to describe rather than to judge, to deal with events rather than personal opinions. A detached, dispassionate, and objective treatment remains the ideal, and serious efforts will be made to comply with this legitimate demand of scholarship despite the inevitable involvement in the issues and problems to be discussed which must colour appraisals made by any individual in the modern world.

The interpretative framework of this study will adhere to a single criterion, the effectiveness of the given action from the viewpoint of Soviet foreign policy. An action which assists the realization of Soviet foreign policy aspirations, is successful; one which does not, is not. Such an evaluative schema implies neither endorsement of a given action nor demurral, simply that it did or did not make a useful contribution to Soviet foreign policy. This frame of reference by no means implies that other grounds for evaluation are not available, are inapplicable, or are incorrect; it is undertaken, in part, to insure against subjective elements influencing the review of activities and events. Doubtless subjective preferences will creep into the study on occasion; but every effort will be made to avoid such lapses.

Throughout the study a distinction will be maintained between religion and Soviet foreign policy. Religion will not be discussed as though it were a component part of the latter, nor as though it were a machination contrived by, or under the absolute dominance of, Soviet policy-makers. Instead, religious institutions and individuals will be approached as independent actors in international affairs who to greater or less degree find it expedient to co-operate with the secular interests of the Soviet State. To be sure, there is little evidence to support or deny such a hypothesis, and there have been voices which would claim that to suggest such a distinction at all is to transmogrify the actual situation,[4] just as others would deny the permissibility of any suggestion whatsoever of congruence between the activities of the Churches and those of the State in international affairs.[5]

Prior to World War II, the participation of the Russian Orthodox Church in Soviet foreign policy was slight.[6] The regime seemed sublimely indifferent to any possible religious dimensions in international life, and only on the rarest of occasions did it permit the Church to render a modicum of service in the international field. Even these attempts by the Church to serve the political interests of the State were most insignificant, with scarcely any discernible impact one way or the other on Soviet foreign policy. Certainly the State gave no evidence of any particular gratitude, but combined its adamant hostility towards religion domestically with an almost complete lack of interest in the Church's offers and rare attempts to render service internationally.

During the first decade of Soviet rule in Russia the impact of religion on Soviet foreign policy was primarily negative. In the Civil

War which erupted almost immediately after the Bolshevik Revolution in 1917 a significant portion of the Orthodox Church joined the White forces, and in areas which were not under the control of the Bolsheviks the foreign armies of intervention enjoyed the vigorous services of the Church, with some clerics going so far as to form military detachments to fight alongside the forces led or supported by foreign interventionists. Patriarch Tikhon, who had been elected Patriarch of Moscow and All Russia immediately after the Bolshevik seizure of power, greeted the new government with outspoken hostility; after 1919 he had to devote no little attention to dissociating himself from the anti-Bolshevik cause in the Civil War.

Despite Tikhon's abandonment of a policy of hostility towards the fledgling Soviet regime in favour of an apolitical approach in 1919, he continued to find himself embroiled in the controversy. The international dimensions of the Russian Orthodox Church at that time caused the Moscow Patriarchate considerable trouble, for in several instances clerics who had fled the country with the collapse of the White armies threatened to involve the mother Church in anti-Soviet sentiments, and on occasion caused the regime a slight degree of embarrassment in international affairs. In December 1921 a group of émigré churchmen met at Karlovtsi, Yugoslavia, and appealed to the European Economic Conference at Genoa for renewed intervention in Russia on religious grounds. Patriarch Tikhon was quick to dissociate himself from these activities.

Even worse, the Karlovtsi group suggested that the Church utilize its considerable store of valuables to effect the overthrow of the government, which was facing a catastrophic famine in the wake of the Civil War. The regime seized upon this indiscretion as confirmation of its ideological thesis that the Church was inherently counter-revolutionary. Already the State had initiated a campaign of expropriation of Church valuables for the aid of the starving, a campaign which was to prove eminently effective in the struggle to reduce the property and popular strength of the Church in Russia. In August 1921 Tikhon had formed a Committee for the Aid of the Starving and appealed to religious leaders in the West for contributions. The State, however, declared the Committee superfluous, and a short time later rejected the Vatican's offer to provide cash subsidies in lieu of confiscation of consecrated religious articles in Russia. The campaign of sequestering Church valuables, which followed, was immensely painful for the Church, seriously weakening its position within the country.

Concurrently, the Living Church adventure began in Russia, a State-approved schism which, although it was soon to prove ephemeral, seemed very serious at the time. No sooner had the schism become established than Patriarch Tikhon was placed under arrest, and the State began to issue publicity in preparation for his forthcoming trial. A vigorous outcry arose in the West, with outspoken protests issuing from Rome, Canterbury, and elsewhere. So intense was the concern that the British threatened to withdraw their trade mission from the USSR. Presumably, it was the seriousness of the international reaction which induced the regime to cancel its plans for the Patriarch, and on 16 June 1923 the Patriarch signed a ' confession ', in return for which he was released. Without necessarily admitting guilt, Tikhon did confess that there were sufficient grounds to warrant juridical action in his case and pledged that ' I am henceforth not an enemy of the Soviet Government.' In particular, he was careful to preclude any future involvements in international intrigues against the USSR: ' I finally and decisively dissociate myself both from foreign and from internal monarchist-White Guard counter-revolution.' [7]

When Tikhon died in 1925, the leadership of the Church came under severe attack, and it soon became apparent that the apolitical stance assumed by Tikhon was no longer sufficient to deter the hostility of the State. One after another, Tikhon's designated successsors were imprisoned, and by 1927 the central administration of the Church was in serious danger of complete disruption. Accordingly, Metropolitan Sergii (Stragorodskii), who had inherited the mantle of leadership when the others senior to him had all been incarcerated—in normal circumstances he would have succeeded the third of Tikhon's successors—decided radically to transform the political policy of the Church. Henceforth the Church under his leadership would pledge unqualified support to the Soviet government in all political matters:

We must show, not in words, but in deeds, that not only people indifferent to Orthodoxy, or those who reject it, can be faithful citizens of the Soviet Union, loyal to the Soviet Government, but also the most fervent adherents of Orthodoxy, to whom it is as dear with all its canonical and liturgical treasures as truth and life. We wish to be Orthodox and at the same time to claim the Soviet Union as our civil motherland, the joys and successes of which are our joys and successes, the misfortunes of which are our misfortunes. Every blow directed against the Union, be it war, boycott, or simply murder from behind a corner, like that in Warsaw [referring to the assassination of the Soviet ambassador by an émigré youth], we acknowledge as a blow directed against us. [8]

It should be noted that Sergii's position offered political support only; all other areas of Church life (tradition, Canon Law, the liturgy, etc.) were to remain sacrosanct and independent. In return, the Church hoped to receive sufficient concessions from the State to allow its continued functioning within Soviet society.

The international ramifications of this change in policy became apparent almost immediately. The Moscow Patriarchate clarified the conditions under which émigré Churches abroad could continue to enjoy the jurisdictional sanction of the mother Church. Included in the stipulations was a pledge of political loyalty:

I, the undersigned, do hereby give the present promise that being now within the jurisdiction of the Moscow Patriarchate, I will not let myself do anything in my public, and particularly in my ecclesiastical, activities that might be taken as an expression of my disloyalty to the Soviet Government.[9]

Obviously, this was a sweeping enough pledge, and perhaps it is understandable that not many Russians enjoying the hospitality of Western countries were quick to pledge allegiance to a foreign government. Metropolitan Evlogii, the Exarch of Western Europe, was deprived of his jurisdiction after he had joined in public prayers for the persecuted Russian Church, and when he was granted jurisdictional sanction by the Ecumenical Patriarch at Constantinople, Sergii protested; on 26 December 1930 Evlogii was officially removed, and Elevferii was appointed Exarch. In 1934 relations with the Karlovtsi Synod were terminated, and the Synod was condemned. On 5 January 1935 Feofil was declared removed from the leadership of the Russian Orthodox Church in America.

Otherwise, opportunities to demonstrate political loyalty to the Soviet government in the international arena were relatively infrequent. In 1930 Sergii was able to render some small, and perhaps inconsequential, service to Soviet foreign interests. With the rise of the antireligious campaign late in the twenties, there were correspondingly greater outcries in the West against the persecution which the Russian Church seemed to be experiencing. The Roman Catholic Church and the Church of England were particularly vigorous in their protests. If Soviet propaganda is to be believed, there was much apprehension in the USSR concerning a ' Pope's Crusade ' against Communism which was imminent. On 18 February 1930 Sergii was unexpectedly allowed to give an interview to foreign journalists in Moscow, in which he took pains to deny the charges which foreign churchmen had been making:

Q : Does persecution of religion really exist in the USSR and what forms does it take?

A : Persecution of religion never did and does not exist in the USSR . . .

Q : Is it true that clergymen and believers undergo repression for their religious convictions, are arrested, exiled, etc.?

A : Repressions which are brought to bear by the Soviet Government in relation to believers and clergymen, befall them by no means for their religious convictions, but in the public sphere, as also for other citizens for various anti-governmental actions . . .

Q : How would you look on material support from abroad and what form might it take?

A : Our position as clergymen is sufficiently guaranteed by the material support of our believers. We consider it morally permissible for us [to receive] our support only from believers. Receiving material support from people of another faith and from outside would be for us a humiliation and would lay on us great moral and perhaps even political obligations and would bind us in our religious activity.[10]

It was obvious from the tone of the conference that Sergii's integrity in adhering to the political platform he had proclaimed in 1927 was unimpeachable, and he and his Church were sincere and blameless in their willingness to co-operate with the political needs of the Soviet State. However, it is questionable whether this exercise was at all successful from the point of view of Soviet foreign policy, for Sergii's statements were at such obvious odds with the actual situation of the Church in the USSR that the only discernible effect in the international reaction to his answers was incredulity, if not outright condemnation of his lack of veracity, or even, perhaps, sheer derision.

In 1931 Sergii rejected the proposal for an ecumenical council suggested by the Ecumenical Patriarchate; *inter alia*, the latter had granted jurisdictional sanction to those in the Russian Orthodox emigration who refused to pledge loyalty to the Soviet government and, furthermore, was engaged in negotiations with the Church of England, one of the most outspoken protesters against Soviet religious policies. In 1935 he condemned the theological work of S. Bulgakov, in Paris, concerning Divine Wisdom; although his objections were eminently theological, Sergii's *ukase* was issued shortly after the Russian Orthodox Theological Institute in Paris, of which Bulgakov was a member, had participated in Anglo-Russian prayers for the persecuted Russian Church.

Otherwise, opportunities to demonstrate willingness to render service to the State in foreign affairs were almost nil during the thirties.

The situation changed radically in 1939. In August, Soviet foreign policy executed the volte face of signing a treaty of non-aggression with Germany; according to a secret protocol Poland was to be partitioned. On 17 September the USSR announced its entry into Eastern Poland. Suddenly the Church inherited an opportunity for service to the regime, for its good offices could be highly useful in support of the Soviet effort among the predominantly Orthodox population there. Two of the remaining four active bishops of the Russian Orthodox Church were dispatched to Eastern Poland and to the Baltic States, when they, too, came under Soviet occupation. Thenceforth until the German invasion of the USSR (22 June 1941), the Church acted in harmony with the State in the newly acquired areas, and was able to render valuable services.

World War II brought immensely increased opportunities to the Church for co-operation with the State. So severe was the crisis of war that the Soviet regime was in critical need of support wherever it might be found. The antireligious campaign was abruptly terminated and the energetic services of the Church were gratefully accepted. While the bulk of the Church's activities were in support of the domestic war effort, an international dimension very quickly developed. Soon the Church was engaged in a broad spectrum of activities. Clerics who had defected to the German occupation forces—e.g. Polycarp in the Ukraine, Sergii (Voskresenskii) in Riga—were condemned; propaganda leaflets were prepared urging resistance behind the German lines, in Rumania, Bulgaria, and elsewhere; interviews were granted to foreign journalists, e.g. Eve Curie; propaganda was issued concerning German war crimes, and the first of what was to become a series of publications intended primarily for foreign consumption (*The Truth about Religion in Russia*, 1942) appeared; contributions were made to Soviet agitation for a Second Front, and to the regime's propaganda against the Catholic Church; and telegrams were sent to Orthodox leaders abroad. A wide area of activity had opened up, which was to grow immensely with the waning of World War II.

On 4 September 1943 Sergii and his two chief subordinates, Nikolai and Aleksii (the future Patriarch), were granted a private audience with Stalin, and the informal concordat between Church and State was ratified. This meeting with Stalin provided the basis for Church-State relations in the USSR from that time onwards. Three days later a *Sobor*

(Council) was called which, after a delay of more than sixteen years, elevated Metropolitan Sergii to Patriarch. The attendance of the Archbishop of York as a guest at the *Sobor* was a harbinger of things to come.

On 15 May 1944 Patriarch Sergii died. The next eight months were spent in preparation for a *Sobor* to elect his successor, which was held from 31 January to 2 February 1945.[11] Aleksii was unanimously elected Patriarch. Fulsome praise was rendered to the Soviet government by the *Sobor*, and the State reciprocated with compliments to the Church duly offered by G. G. Karpov, the Chairman of the newly formed Council for the Affairs of the Russian Orthodox Church attached to the Council of People's Commissars. Patterns for future activity could be clearly discerned in the *Sobor*, for an impressive array of visiting dignitaries was present as invited guests, with travel provided by the Soviet State. Among them were the Patriarchs of Antioch and Alexandria, representatives of the Patriarchs of Constantinople, Jerusalem, Rumania, and Serbia, and the Metropolitan of the patriarchal jurisdiction of the Russian Orthodox Church of America. The *Sobor* gave convincing demonstration of the Church's ability to exercise an influence on foreign churchmen, and of its willingness to support the political government in its activities. Obviously, a programme of international activities was under consideration.

2 Consolidation of Hegemony

THE modern history of the role of religion in Soviet foreign policy began on 10 April 1945. On that date Stalin, together with Molotov, was visited by the leaders of the Russian Orthodox Church, the newly enthroned Patriarch Aleksii, Metropolitan Nikolai, and the priest Kolchitskii. From this time forward the Russian Orthodox Church (and, later, other religious denominations in the USSR) would initiate a vastly expanded programme of international activities, conducted in the closest harmony with the foreign policy goals of the Soviet Union.[1]

At the time the Soviet State was about to initiate a vigorous foreign policy, and for the next three years it would enjoy the greatest expansion in its history. The war was rapidly drawing to a close, with Soviet armies rolling through Eastern Europe, converging on Berlin. Stalin had just returned from the Yalta Conference, at which he had secured from the Allied Powers a division of the formerly occupied areas into spheres of influence, and in the vacuum caused by the collapse of the Third Reich, the Soviet State could expect to extend its influence immensely. The creation of an empire of aligned nations under the leadership of the USSR was imminent, and as yet there was no clear demarcation of the range to which such a sphere of influence could be extended by a vigorous and intelligently executed foreign policy.

For its part, the Russian Church could envisage a marked contribution to the forthcoming endeavours of the State. Much of the expansion of Soviet hegemony would take place in areas with a large Orthodox population. During the months between the partitioning of Poland in 1939 and the German invasion of Russia, and again as the occupying forces were driven westwards, the Russian Orthodox Church had gained experience and demonstrated its competence in contributing to the consolidation of Soviet rule. In the Baltic States and in the newly acquired areas of what had been Eastern Poland, the predominantly Orthodox population had been brought under the wing of the Moscow Patriarchate. In the Orthodox areas of Eastern Europe—Rumania, Bulgaria, and parts of Yugoslavia—the Church might similarly serve in providing leadership to ensure that Soviet interests would meet minimal opposition from the powerful Churches; while in the non-Orthodox areas—Hungary, Poland, East Germany, and, ultimately,

16

Czechoslovakia and Albania—the Orthodox Churches could be given maximum support, allowing them to chart the path for and, hopefully, reduce somewhat the influence of the dominant Catholic, Protestant, or (in the case of Albania) Muslim religious institutions. If Soviet control should be extended beyond the limits of the Red Army's occupation, Russian Orthodoxy could hope to provide an auxiliary, but nevertheless useful, facility for Soviet influence in the existing Orthodox Churches, to the East through Manchuria to China and even Japan, to the South in the Orthodox Patriarchates of the Middle East, and to the West in the Orthodox émigré communities of Western Europe. Even in areas in which there was no hope of extending Soviet hegemony, such as Great Britain and the United States, the Russian Church could render a small service by influencing the Orthodox minorities—as well as the Churches in general—in the hope of blunting the inevitable resistance to Soviet expansion which would arise.

How much of this coming campaign of international activities was discussed at the meeting with Stalin, and in what detail, has not, of course, been released for public consumption.[2] According to Aleksii's report, domestic matters were discussed, but inasmuch as the forthcoming visit of Russian Orthodox leaders to Jerusalem was also mentioned, and especially in view of the vigorous international Church activity which commenced almost immediately, it would be reasonable to suppose that the meeting between the leaders of State and Church ratified the basic outlines, at least, of the Church's coming contribution to Soviet foreign policy.

Almost immediately, the plan to secure hegemony over the Orthodox Churches in areas of Soviet occupation was placed in operation, and in the five years following World War II the Moscow Patriarchate emerged as the unquestioned leader of Orthodoxy in Eastern Europe.

The Churches of the predominantly Orthodox Balkan States were quick to affiliate with Moscow. Bulgaria was visited by Grigorii, then Archbishop of Pskov, who was to prove second only to Metropolitan Nikolai in implementing the foreign policy of the Moscow Patriarchate. Exarch Stefan, the head of the Bulgarian Orthodox Church, visited Moscow in June 1945, and Patriarch Aleksii returned the visit the following year. Stefan's successor, Metropolitan Kirill, soon to be elevated to Patriarch (the first in Bulgarian history), visited Moscow in July 1950.

Especially close relations were established with the Rumanian Orthodox Church. Almost immediately after the meeting with Stalin,

Bishop Yeronim of Kishinev and Moldavia was sent to Rumania, and during the next half decade the Rumanian Patriarch and his successor made five separate visits to Moscow. Patriarch Aleksii visited Bucharest in 1947, and, interestingly enough, the staff of the Russian Embassy attended his liturgy in the Rumanian patriarchal cathedral.

As for Yugoslavia, Bishop Sergii of Kirovgrad was delegated to secure the co-operation of the Serbian Orthodox Church. He accomplished his mission with dispatch, visiting Marshal Tito, and receiving medals from the Yugoslav government for himself and Aleksii. One of the host bishops stated during his visit, ' It is necessary to agree that among all the nations professing the Orthodox faith, only the Russian nation can stand at the head of historic Orthodoxy.' [3] The harmonious relationship between the Serbian and Moscow Patriarchates was to be short-lived, however; with the rupture between the USSR and Yugoslavia and the latter's expulsion from the Cominform, the Moscow Patriarchate broke off relations and returned the medals given by Tito, and it was not until the *rapprochement* with Yugoslavia, under Khrushchev, that ecclesiastical relations between the two Patriarchates were resumed.

Similarly, in the non-Orthodox portions of the new Soviet empire, Russian Orthodoxy made a contribution to the establishment of Soviet suzerainty. Harmonious relations were established with the minority Orthodox Church in Poland, which was eventually granted autocephaly by the Moscow Patriarchate (a prerogative which the Ecumenical Patriarch in Istanbul considered his alone), with a Russian national, Makarii (Oleksiuk) as its Metropolitan. The Hungarian Orthodox parishes, which had petitioned to be received into the jurisdiction of the Moscow Patriarchate in 1945, were accepted by the latter in 1949, over the protests of the Ecumenical Patriarchate, to which these parishes had belonged. In Czechoslovakia the Orthodox Church requested and was granted a Russian Exarch in 1946, and, incongruously, was visited by G. G. Karpov, Chairman of the Soviet governmental Council for the Affairs of the Russian Orthodox Church that same year. In 1951 the Czechoslovak Church was granted autocephalous status by the Moscow Patriarchate, again despite the protests of the Ecumenical Patriarch. In Germany the émigré Russian Orthodox community, which had been vociferously anti-Communist during the inter-war period and which had enthusiastically supported Hitler as a crusader against ' godless Communism,' quickly submitted to Muscovite jurisdiction (although in West Germany the Russian émigrés rejected this affiliation and reorganized themselves into the independent Russian Orthodox Synod Abroad).

Orthodox minorities in non-Christian areas were also brought into the fold. The small Albanian Orthodox Church was granted rather dubious autocephaly after some delay, while the Russian Orthodox Church in Manchuria almost immediately accepted Muscovite jurisdiction, despite the fact that before World War II Harbin had served as a centre of anti-Soviet émigré sentiments. With the victory of the Chinese revolution, the Orthodox Churches of China also reverted to the jurisdiction of the Moscow Patriarchate.

Thus throughout the area of direct Soviet control the Church cooperated to the extent to which it was able in facilitating the establishment and consolidation of Soviet influence. By ensuring that the Orthodox religious communities were subject to the ecclesiastical leadership of the Moscow Patriarchate, the latter was able to make a useful, if sometimes marginal, contribution to the implementation of Soviet policy in these areas.

The Moscow Patriarchate enjoyed rather less achievement with regard to the Churches on what were to become the borders of the Soviet area. There seemed little chance of success with the Orthodox Church of Greece and with the Ecumenical Patriarchate in Turkey, and, indeed, the Moscow Patriarchate devoted no effort at all to futile attempts to gain influence over these Churches. Serious negotiations were conducted with the Orthodox Church of Finland, but, as the cold war developed, only minimal results were achieved. Similarly, opportunities for extension of influence over the Orthodox Church of Japan were not especially promising, at least for so long as the US should enjoy overwhelming influence there.

The major efforts of the Russian Orthodox Church immediately after the meeting with Stalin were devoted to the Middle East, and here considerable success was achieved. In the areas of Soviet occupation, where there could be little doubt of acceptance of Muscovite ecclesiastical leadership, the negotiations were handled, by and large, by subordinates; in the Middle East, however, Patriarch Aleksii himself initiated the attempt to extend the influence of the Russian Orthodox Church, ably assisted by Metropolitan Nikolai, who for the next fifteen years would serve as the Church's chief representative in foreign affairs. Aleksii, Nikolai, and the repented schismatic, Archbishop Vitalii, embarked on 28 May 1945, a fortnight after the capitulation of

Germany, on the voyage which, *inter alia*, had been discussed in the meeting with Stalin.

The first stop was the Holy Land. Because this was the first time that a Russian Patriarch had visited Jerusalem, the event attracted considerable publicity, and the Soviet State, by supplying an aircraft piloted by a Hero of the Soviet Union for the delegation, publicly demonstrated its approval of the ecclesiastical attempt to build relations with the Churches of the Middle East. In the meetings with the Patriarch of Jerusalem partial, but by no means total, success was achieved. Plagued by low income due, in part, to the tensions between a Greek hierarchy presiding over a predominantly Arab church constituency, the Patriarchate of Jerusalem was not completely uninterested in a possible resumption of the financial aid which had been received from Russia before 1917. Indeed, some subsidies were forthcoming a short while after Aleksii's initial visit. Contacts with the Russian émigré communities in Jerusalem were less felicitous, but the visiting delegation was able to weather such hostility as it encountered. Finally, in the next few years the Moscow Patriarchate regained title to certain of the properties which had belonged to the Russian Church before 1917, and, ultimately, was able to re-establish its permanent mission in Jerusalem.

Egypt, where Patriarch Aleksii enjoyed good success, was next on the itinerary. Especially warm relations were established with the Patriarch of Alexandria, who agreed to accompany the delegation from Moscow for the remainder of the trip through the Middle East. Patriarch Aleksii was received by King Farouk, and also succeeded in bringing the churches of the Russian émigré colony in Egypt under the jurisdiction of the Moscow Patriarchate.

Without Metropolitan Nikolai, who departed for England, Patriarch Aleksii and his party then visited Beirut including, as was the custom, the local Soviet Embassy in the itinerary. Apparently the visit was uneventful, but nevertheless important, if only for the fact that the Orthodox, comprising less than half the population of Lebanon, because of historical circumstances retain much of the country's governmental power.

Damascus, reached next, was a more fruitful visit. The Syrian Orthodox Church, Arab in its composition, was not on close terms with Greek Churches, and suffered from chronic and acute poverty. The Patriarch of Antioch was thus most amenable to re-establishing relations with the Russian Church, which before 1917 had provided welcome financial relief, and, when Russian subsidies were again forthcoming as a result of Aleksii's visit, he served for several years as one of the Moscow Patriarchate's more reliable supporters in the Middle East.

After brief visits to Tehran and Baghdad, Patriarch Aleksii and his party returned to the USSR, concluding an extended foreign visit which secured for the Russian Orthodox Church a powerful voice in the religious affairs of the Middle East. Should the Soviet State expand in a southerly direction, not a completely unlikely possibility in view of the imminent British withdrawal from Iran, the influence which the Russian Church had gained in the Middle East might serve as a welcome adjunct to the implementation of State policy in the area.

The Moscow Patriarchate's opportunities for making a contribution to Soviet foreign policy were much more limited in the Western world. With non-Orthodox Christianity predominant, together with the high degree of secularization which had already occurred in these societies, Russian Orthodoxy had only the smallest of opportunities to gain immediate, direct influence. Nevertheless, during the brief period between the conclusion of World War II and the rise of the cold war, when it was not yet clear how far the western boundary of Soviet influence would extend and before serious opposition had arisen, the Russian Church could make a marginal contribution to Soviet foreign policy in the West.

The establishment of jurisdictional authority over the émigré Russian Church in Germany, which was quickly reversed in areas not subject to Soviet occupation, has already been mentioned. The Russian Church came much closer to success, however, in France.

As one of the major recipients of the post-Revolutionary wave of emigration from Russia, France maintained a sizeable community of Russian Orthodox émigrés. Particularly in the immediate post-war period, when memories of the wartime alliance remained strong and when the Communist Party, enjoying much respect for its contribution to the resistance movements against the Germans, was vigorous and was even represented in the government, there was a considerable desire within the Russian emigration in France to reaffiliate with the Russian Church. Inasmuch as it seemed within the bounds of possibility—even if rather unlikely—that the Communist Party might succeed in rising to power in France, any influence which the Moscow Patriarchate might gain in the Russian community there would serve as a most welcome adjunct to future Soviet relations with the country.

Hence the Patriarchate was quick to respond to the request of the aged leader of the Russian Church in France, Metropolitan Evlogii, to be received back into the jurisdiction of the mother Church. (The Moscow Patriarchate, it will be recalled, had severed relations with the French émigré Church in 1930 because of the latter's refusal to pledge allegiance to the Soviet government; in the interim, the Ecumenical Patriarchate had provided jurisdictional sanction.) Metropolitan Nikolai was sent to Paris, and on his arrival on 24 August 1945 was met at the airport by a large delegation, including the Soviet Ambassador and the commanding general of the Soviet military mission, as well as by many churchmen.[4] He enjoyed immediate success in reaching agreement with Evlogii for the immediate return to Muscovite jurisdiction (curiously enough, there was no requirement of repentance, which in other circumstances would be expected of a bishop whose canonical relations with his superiors had been severed). Evlogii was not confident, however, that he could bring all his parishes with him, so Nikolai devoted considerable effort to persuading the parishioners, painting a glowing picture of the condition of the Church in the USSR. There was much opposition, but apparently Nikolai's mission was successful and the Russian Orthodox Church in France was welcomed back to Muscovite jurisdiction.

It would seem that this transfer of jurisdiction was accomplished rather too hastily, for permission first had to be received from the Ecumenical Patriarch, who had appointed Evlogii his Exarch, before such a transfer could take effect. Nikolai led Evlogii to believe that this matter had already been arranged, but in fact it had not, and ultimately the entire scheme would be frustrated on the grounds of this canonical irregularity.

While in Paris Nikolai also secured the submission of the smaller émigré Orthodox Church which before the war had belonged to the militantly anti-Communist but canonically prestigious Karlovtsi orientation. Metropolitan Serafim, the leader of this émigré Church in France, agreed to return to Muscovite jurisdiction, albeit in a somewhat curious manner. According to one report, Serafim's first meeting with Nikolai was rather hostile, Serafim responding to Nikolai's overtures with highly embarrassing questions regarding the fate of numerous Russian bishops who had disappeared during the inter-war period in Russia. A second meeting was held in private, however, after which Serafim was willing to accept the jurisdiction of the Moscow Patriarchate, and thereafter he seemed a most loyal servant of the mother Church. This abrupt reversal of position gave rise to speculation as to whether pressure had been applied during this second meeting, for Serafim, whose anti-Communist attitudes had been so vehement that he supported the Germans even during the occupation period in France, was not in an especially enviable position in liberated France, where anti-Nazi and anti-collaborationist feelings were still strong.

One other aspect of Nikolai's mission was less successful. While in Paris he made moving appeals to the émigré Russians, seeking to persuade them to end their long exile and return to the homeland. A small number of the émigrés did return, some to enjoy long and relatively untroubled careers in the Church in the USSR.

In large measure Nikolai's fortnight in Paris was a resounding success, and, after being received at the Soviet Embassy, he returned to Moscow on 5 September.

The relations of the Russian Orthodox Church with Britain and the United States were somewhat less crucial for Soviet foreign policy, for by no stretch of the imagination could these countries be expected to come into the Soviet field of influence in the immediate future. Nevertheless, even in the waning days of World War II it took no special clairvoyance to foresee the confrontation which the cold war would bring sooner or later, and the Church could render some small service in tempering at least some of the inevitable hostility which would arise in these countries.

England was of particular importance, for before the war the English Churches had been most vociferous in their denunciation of the Soviet regime's treatment of the Churches, and, on occasion, this opposition was sufficient to cause pre-war Soviet foreign policy a degree of embarrassment. Hence Nikolai was dispatched to England half-way through the Patriarch's Middle East journey, and, while in England, he made a great and lasting impression, creating much good will in his audience with the King, his visits to the Archbishop of Canterbury, and his conversations with other religious leaders. He did not succeed in persuading the émigré Russian Orthodox to reaffiliate with Moscow, but the Russian Church in England was exceedingly small, and this failure was more than cancelled out by Nikolai's immense success in building a favourable image for the post-war Russian Church and, less directly, for the beneficent government of the USSR.

To judge by the conduct of the negotiations, it would not appear that the Russian Church in the United States ranked very high on the agenda of the Moscow Patriarchate, even though there was every indication that spectacular success might be achieved. It was clear by the end of the war that the US and the USSR would be the centres of power in the post-war world, with Germany destroyed, France demoralized, Great Britain exhausted, and the European colonial powers losing their overseas possessions. As a result the State may have advised rather more caution in the Patriarchate's relations with the US. Certainly these negotiations were not conducted with the broad latitude, finesse, and dispatch which brought so much success to the Church elsewhere in the world.

The Russian Orthodox Church in America was large, vigorous, and comparatively well integrated into society, with roots which had been established long before the wave of emigration following the Revolution. Because of its unwillingness to pledge loyalty to the Soviet government, relations with the Russian Church in America had been severed, and prior to World War II the American Church had been under the jurisdiction of the Karlovtsi Synod. The Russian community in America had entered whole-heartedly into the spirit of the wartime alliance, however, and had severed relations with the Synod because of its support of Hitler's ' Crusade against Communism '. As a result, the Russian Church in America was without any canonical jurisdictional affiliation whatsoever, and appealed to Moscow for recognition as an Autonomous Church under the Patriarch's jurisdiction. This presented the Moscow Patriarchate with an exceedingly promising opportunity for gaining influence over a large, active, and strategically located Church in the West.

The negotiations, however, were a comedy of errors. The Americans were invited to send a delegation to the *Sobor* of 1945, and then because of visa restrictions and bureaucratic obstruction (they were made to transfer from air to rail transportation for the journey across Siberia) they were able to arrive in Moscow only after the *Sobor* had concluded. The representative sent to America, Archbishop Aleksii of Yaroslavl and Rostov, was apparently not the most politic of men, and made many enemies by his unsubtle attempts to seize power. The Patriarchate unequivocally insisted that the American Church pledge loyalty to the Soviet government, despite the vigorous pleas that the Orthodox in America, many of them third and fourth generation American citizens, could scarcely pledge allegiance to a foreign government. Even when a large Council of the Russian Church in America met at Cleveland, Ohio, in 1946 and voted to affiliate with Moscow over the objections of the leadership, the Patriarchate responded coldly, finally sending Metropolitan Grigorii to the US with the demand that his decisions be accepted without question and that the Moscow Patriarchate retain power to veto any candidate chosen by the Americans as their leader, for any reason whatsoever. At a late stage in the proceedings, Moscow relented somewhat and appeared to be willing to accept the autonomy of the American Church, but then insisted that Archbishop Makarii, who had been excommunicated by the Russian Orthodox Church in America for affiliating uncanonically with Moscow some months earlier, be accepted as the head of the American Church. Perhaps most important, the negotiations were not conducted with that rapidity which had characterized other areas of the Moscow Patriarchate's foreign activities, but were allowed to drag along until the favourable auspices had dissipated and the hostilities of the cold war had begun to penetrate into the Russian community in America. As a result, the entire episode came to nothing, and the negotiations collapsed without result.

The initial success of the Russian Church's service to Soviet foreign policy was severely inhibited by the results which were quickly forthcoming from the aggressiveness of the Soviet Union in the post-war world. The Church had demonstrated its considerable ability to win friends in non-Soviet areas, and was well on the way to establishing centres of Russian interest in many countries where Soviet power had not yet prevailed. With very few exceptions, these initial successes came to naught, however, victims of the general erosion of friendship and trust which Soviet foreign policy engendered. The border clashes in Iran, the civil war in Greece, and, finally, the Berlin blockade and the *coup d'état* in Czechoslovakia in 1948 served to give notice to the rest of the world that the euphoria of the wartime alliance was over, and the world began to gird itself for serious conduct of the cold war.

In such circumstances, the Church could scarely expect to preserve the fruits of its efforts in international affairs. The American negotiations had failed. In France, after Evlogii died in 1946, the efforts of the Moscow Patriarchate to salvage the situation were fruitless, and the Russian Orthodox Church in France reverted to the jurisdiction of the Ecumenical Patriarchate. Some residual benefits remained in England, where the goodwill elicited by Nikolai during his visit would prove durable, and in the Middle East, where Russian subsidies were still welcomed in certain ecclesiastical quarters. No further headway could be made with the Finnish or the Japanese Orthodox after the world situation had crystallized, however.

In view of the rapidly changing political climate in the later forties, it is scarcely surprising that the Church's boldest attempt to expand its influence was a failure. In 1947 and 1948 the Moscow Patriarchate made a powerful bid to wrest pre-eminence in the entire Orthodox world away from the Ecumenical Patriarch of Constantinople.

Themes of aggrandizement were certainly not foreign to Russian Orthodoxy. As early as the fifteenth century, the theory of ' Moscow, the Third Rome ' had been formulated in the Russian Church, which postulated that just as the barbarian invasions had caused the centre of Christianity to shift from Rome to Constantinople, so the Turkish invasion had deposed the ' Second Rome '; Moscow was destined to be the Third Rome, and ' a fourth Rome there will not be.' In the im-mediate post-war world, advocates of the Russian Church could make a powerful case for Russian leadership of the Orthodox world. The Russian nation had emerged from World War II as one of the two greatest powers in the world. Russian Orthodoxy was overwhelmingly the largest Church, and if the depredations of the thirties had reduced its hierarchy to an insignificant number by no means commensurate with its millions of adherents, this oversight was being corrected with all haste. Particularly after the concordat with the Soviet State, the Russian Church was the richest of all Orthodox Churches, seemingly able to give limitless emoluments to those whom it favoured. When compared with the Ecumenical Patriarchate, which was poor and with few parishes, and which was enduring its fifth century of existence in a Muslim country, an impressive case could be made that leadership belonged to Moscow, *de jure* as well as *de facto*.

Obviously, for the Russian Church to win pre-eminence over the entire Orthodox world would be of significant interest for the foreign policy of the Soviet State. Immense opportunities would become avail-able for influencing countries with sizeable Orthodox Churches, offer-ing to the Soviet practitioners of foreign policy an exceedingly useful adjunct to the more normal channels of political persuasion.

Accordingly, the Moscow Patriarchate in 1947 made the bold manoeuvre of unilaterally proposing that an eighth Ecumenical Council be convened, the first since the Council of Nicaea in 787. Such a coun-cil would be an event of the first magnitude in the history of Orthodoxy, and in making the proposal the Moscow Patriarchate was arrogating to itself the position of *primus inter pares* in all the Orthodox Pat-riarchates. To some degree, it is not unlikely that such an attempt to gain hegemony was envisaged in the planning of Patriarch Aleksii's tour of the Orthodox Middle East, for his failure to visit the Ecumenical Patriarchate at Istanbul was a studied omission.

Not unpredictably, the Ecumenical Patriarch immediately responded with a vigorous protest that, by tradition and Canon Law, only he has the right to call an Ecumenical Council, and in making the attempt the Moscow Patriarch was openly usurping authority. The Ecumenical Patriarch had powerful support from the Greek Orthodox Church, for the Moscow Patriarchate's rather unsubtle attempts to intervene on behalf of the Communist partisans in the civil war were not especially welcome in Greece.

As a result, the plan to hold an Ecumenical Council in Moscow was abandoned. In its place, invitations were sent to all the Orthodox Primates to attend the celebration of the 500th anniversary of the autocephaly of the Russian Orthodox Church in 1948, after which a conference would be held for discussion of common problems. Obviously, the Moscow Patriarchate, unsuccessful in gaining pre-eminence over the Orthodox world *de jure* by calling an Ecumenical Council, had aspirations of gaining that position *de facto* by convening a conference which would be an Ecumenical Council in everything but name.

The celebration was duly held in July 1948 but the results were disappointing.[5] The Patriarchs and canonical leaders of those Churches which were under immediate Soviet political domination were all present. For the rest the Ecumenical Patriarch, the Greek Church, and the Patriarchate of Antioch sent only representatives. The Patriarch of Alexandria sent no delegates but agreed that the Antiochene delegation should represent him, and the Patriarchate of Jerusalem was absent altogether. Furthermore, the delegations representing the Ecumenical Patriarchate and the Greek Church attended the celebration only, refusing to attend the conference which followed. In actual fact, the *Sobor* of 1945 had attracted a more imposing list of Orthodox visitors, and could with less inaccuracy have been called a council with ecumenical representation than could the gathering of 1948.

Nevertheless, the meeting was held with much ceremony and splendour. Karpov, representing the Soviet State, took an active part in the proceedings. The Serbian Patriarch openly called the gathering an Ecumenical Council, and at the conference a number of issues were discussed—relations with Roman Catholicism, the validity of Anglican ordination, the Church calendar, the ecumenical movement. An impressive degree of consensus was achieved, but many of the resolutions passed by the conference bore such a noticeable imprint of secular, rather than purely ecclesiastical, motivation that the religious impact of the meeting was largely vitiated. In particular, great emphasis was given to the contrast between the Orthodox East, where peace and human justice prevail (thanks in large measure to the advent of the Communist form of structuring social life), and the warlike and exploiting Protestant and Catholic West. As a result, any hopes which might have been entertained that the conference could wrest even *de facto* leadership over Orthodoxy from the Ecumenical Patriarchate were frustrated; the event served to demonstrate that the Russian Church was able to exert effective influence over certain Orthodox Churches, primarily in Eastern Europe, and could attract considerable publicity and produce ecclesiastical formulations acceptable to the requirements of Soviet foreign policy, but little else.

The celebration of 1948 marked the close of the initial phase of the participation of the Russian Church in Soviet foreign policy, reflecting a metamorphosis which was taking place in the larger designs of the State. The period of expansion had drawn to a close for the USSR. The vacuum of power resulting from World War II had now been filled, with Soviet influence extending to the demarcation line drawn through Europe, and with Western Europe well on the way to recovery. The aggressiveness which had characterized Soviet foreign policy immediately after World War II could not long be ignored, and the US had re-entered the European theatre in force with the Marshall Plan and other forms of direct and indirect support. The Greek war, the Berlin blockade, and the Czech *coup d'état* had occasioned a definite reversal of American disarmament, and the political map of the world had assumed a shape which would remain largely unaltered for the foreseeable future.

With the hardening of the political situation, Soviet foreign policy gradually evolved away from expansion and towards a more defensive posture. The rapid accumulation of military power by the US, which still enjoyed sole possession of atomic weapons and vast superiority in air power, was a formidable obstacle to Soviet expansionist designs, and prudence was indicated, at least until the Soviet economy could close the armaments gap. In foreign policy, Stalin's preference for a 'continental' approach became dominant. The US, with its naval and air superiority, was already a global power, able to exert its influence despite geographical obstacles. For the remainder of the Stalin period, the USSR would content itself with seeking contiguous expansion only, largely ignoring opportunities which might present themselves in areas not adjacent to the Soviet empire.

With the change in the international situation, the foreign affairs of the Russian Church, predicated as they had been on an expansionist phase of State policy, were virtually bankrupt. The division of the world into two armed camps had nullified nearly every initial success achieved by the Church in non-Soviet areas, while within the Soviet sphere of influence, the establishment of Soviet control over Eastern Europe was proceeding well; the influence of the Moscow Patriarchate remained useful, but it was no longer quite so important. Unless some alternative sphere of service could be discovered, it appeared that the period of the Russian Orthodox Church's usefulness to Soviet foreign policy had drawn to a close.

3 The Cold War

A NEW dimension of Soviet foreign policy was already developing, one which would offer religion a revitalized role in assisting the State. In a world exhausted by the trauma of war, Stalin as early as 1946 had suggested that the desire for peace should be fashioned into an anti-Western instrument, and other spokesmen had followed suit. Accordingly, Soviet initiatives bore fruit at a meeting in 1948 at Wroclaw in Poland, and early in 1949 the World Peace Council was formed. This organization became the leading force in an institutionalized, co-ordinated progaganda campaign which for the next several years was to serve as an important instrument in the implementation of Soviet foreign policy, and from its inception the Russian Church made a significant contribution to the peace campaign.[1]

The organized peace movement was fashioned primarily as a defensive weapon. By focusing maximum attention on the peace issue, as interpreted from a Soviet point of view, to some degree public opinion could be swayed in such a manner as to inhibit contrary activities by governments which depended, wholly or in part, on the support of their constituencies. In particular, such sentiment could be mobilized in support of the chief goals of Soviet foreign policy during the defensive period necessitated by the military imbalance: inhibiting Western rearmament and frustrating attempts to form military alliances in the West. In addition, because one need not be a Communist to participate willingly in the Soviet peace effort, the movement could serve to extend the influence of the Cominform and other Soviet-oriented international organizations somewhat beyond the limited circle of convinced Communists, engaging a number of non-Communist but pacifistic individuals and groups in the effort.

The Church could make a large contribution to this area of Soviet foreign policy. Because the Church claimed to be above politics, and in many circles this claim was accepted, its participation could provide the peace campaign with an aura of legitimacy which would be difficult to achieve otherwise. Furthermore, the Church could expand the movement's influence by attracting certain Western churchmen, and by mobilizing the deep and eminently legitimate stream of pacifism throughout the Christian world in support of the campaign. The most vivid illustration of this latter area of service occurred in May 1952 when the Moscow Patriarchate convened a large conference of religious leaders from all denominations and religions in the USSR. The results of the conference, unanimous in supporting the USSR's promotion of peace and in condemning the aggression of the West, were highly publicized, with the proceedings handsomely presented in several languages for distribution in the West.

The basic theme of the peace campaign was anti-Western propaganda. During this period Soviet propaganda was not, perhaps, a model of subtlety, and Metropolitan Nikolai, who was to be the chief spokesman for the Russian Orthodox Church throughout the campaign, demonstrated his ability to work with the idiom at the First USSR Conference for Peace in August, 1949 :

And thus, at a time when our country and the people's Democracies are engaged in peaceful construction and are bending all their will and effort in that direction, common people the world over are alarmed by the ring of a knife, rusty with human blood, as it is sharpened by the hand of a murderer. Death is again raising its ruthless scythe over the fields of the earth, preparing to reap a bountiful harvest. The same dark forces that ten years ago hurled humanity into the abyss of indescribable suffering, again wish to hold a blood feast, for, being born to feed on human blood, they cannot live without it . . .

The transatlantic octopus is trying to fasten its greedy tentacles around the whole globe. Capitalist America, the rabid fornicatress of resurrected Babylon, having set up a world market, is trying to seduce the people of the world while pushing them toward war. But the common people of all countries are turning their eyes away from her shameless nakedness with a feeling of abomination. None of them are, or can be, enticed. Only those succumb to seduction, who barter away their country and who, in all justice, can be called nothing but sworn enemies of their people.

The transatlantic sirens sing of ' liberty '. But only a man with a black conscience and a clouded intellect can say that liberty exists in a country where people are lynched, where children are kidnapped, where tear [gas] bombs are thrown at workers, that is, at the people who create the country's wealth, where grain is burned in the sight of the hungry, where those who endeavour to restore to the word ' liberty ' its true meaning are flung into jail, where gold is minted for the purchase of accomplices in other countries and guns are cast in order to drench in human blood the peaceful valleys of Greece, China, Indonesia and Viet-Nam. Liberty to rob, coerce and slaughter—such is their ' liberty '! [2]

Among the specific issues of the peace propaganda, armaments, particularly atomic weapons, occupied a large place. For example, in

1954, well after the USSR had announced success in effecting a thermo-
nuclear explosion, Nikolai proclaimed:

When the hydrogen bomb was exploded on Bikini and the fatal consequences of this explosion were marked, all the peoples of our planet were
indignant in spirit, but they did not fall into despair. The experiment with
the hydrogen bomb evoked not fear but protest . . .

If, before the explosion of the hydrogen bomb, many among the people
had already nourished several illusions relating to its moral consequences
on intended antagonists, in view of the terrible and unforeseen consequences of this explosion, the people of all nations, religions and persuasions understood the danger to which all mankind and its culture is
subjected.

. . . Powerful waves of protest rush about the face of the whole earth
requiring the immediate prohibition of atomic and hydrogen weapons for
which the Russian Orthodox Church has loudly been raising its voice
during all the recent years.[3]

Even though the US no longer possessed a monopoly, until delivery
systems could be developed and sufficient quantities of strategic
weapons accumulated, the USSR's military power was designed for
conventional warfare, and the peace campaign's agitation against
weapons of mass destruction was eminently suitable to the requirements
of Soviet foreign policy, provided opprobrium was not allowed to attach
to the East along with the West.

With the beginning of the Korean War in 1950, the peace campaign
came into its own. That war, in which UN forces were directly engaged
while the USSR was involved only indirectly was ideally suited for the
particular sort of propaganda of which the peace campaign was capable.
Indeed, possession of a mobilized, functioning agency for propaganda
when the war began was of immense benefit to Soviet foreign policy.
The Church contributed to the propaganda effort with enthusiasm:

Yet another circumstance of the Korean events is well known, and it is to
this circumstance that I wish to draw your attention. I have in mind the
methods the American aggressors are using to conduct the war in Korea.

.   .   .   .

We see, then, that the spirit and the flesh of fascism have not disappeared,
that there are some who are continuing the delirious dreams of the fanatic
Hitler and are attempting to make them come true.

The followers have nothing to learn from their teachers.

No sooner had they begun their criminal aggression than the American
neo-fascists began the planned, cannibalistic extermination of the
' inferior ' Korean race.

What do we see?

Brazen flouting not only of the norms of international law but of all standards of human morality. Executions without trial or investigation, held in secret and in public. Terrible mutilation of victims: they cut off ears, noses and breasts, gouge out eyes, break arms and legs, crucify patriots, bury women and infants alive, and so on. Revival of the customs of savages—they scalp Korean patriots for ' souvenirs.'

To exterminate the population the American criminals first of all fiendishly slaughtered political prisoners (from 200,000 to 400,000 people), forcing them to dig their own graves beforehand; the bodies of the patriots who were hanged or shot or who died from typhus were flung into a ravine, and the cliff blown up to cover the traces of the crime. The barbaric bombing of peaceful towns and villages has been carried out solely for the purpose of annihilating the civilian population.

.   .   .   .

These representatives of the ' superior ' race have been and are committing mass rape of Korean women and girls, herding them from surrounding villages, making them drunk on gin and raping them. Not stopping at such outrage, in some places they drove the unfortunates into tunnels which they blew up after machine-gunning the victims.[4]

When the germ warfare campaign began in 1952, the Church was not reluctant to contribute to the general propaganda on this theme as well.

One particular contribution which the Church was able to make to the peace propaganda was to implicate the Western Churches in the general guilt. Among the aggressors in Korea were ' leaders of Christian organizations ' who ' know the Bible and quite frequently announce this fact for all to hear '.[5] Western Christians were exhorted to rise up against such leaders in defence of peace. A perennial target of Soviet propaganda, the Roman Catholic Church received much attention from the Church in the peace campaign:

We consider it blasphemous trampling of the most fundamental principles of Christianity when we see how the Christian religion, with the collusion of its high Catholic representatives, is being unscrupulously used in the class interests of the capitalist rulers of Europe and America, to help oppress and exploit the working masses and to pave the way for another bloody shambles.

The Pope revealed his anti-Christian face in all its spiritual ugliness by his recent decree excommunicating Communists and those who sympathize with the latter, the decree which fundamentally contradicts the basic principles of the Christian Gospel and which came into being in consequence of the beastly malice harboured by the head of the Roman Catholic Church.[6]

A second specific service rendered by the Church was in narrowing the definition of pacifism, and particularly of Christian pacifism. It was axiomatic in the propaganda that the only genuine aspiration for peace was that which expressed itself in the specific terms of the Soviet approach to the subject. Any other attempt to find a solution to the problem of war, and particularly failure to participate in the Soviet-sponsored peace movement, implied, covertly or overtly, immoral support of Western aggression. The Church extended this limitation by asserting that no Christian could be a pacifist—nor, indeed, even a genuine Christian—unless he supported this particular form of the struggle for peace. In connection with the germ warfare campaign, Nikolai addressed Christians of the West with the categorical statement,

All religious people without exception must support the Appeal of the Bureau of the World Peace Council . . .

Since there are no worshippers of evil and falsehood among us, we cannot have different opinions regarding our common need of peace, nor can there be any dispute among us concerning the means of achieving it.[7]

The peace campaign was a successful and effective instrument of Soviet foreign policy, especially after the Korean War began. With an active war in progress and the danger of an expanded conflagration imminent, a natural wave of apprehension rose throughout the world, which could be exploited by peace propaganda. The World Peace Council and its subsidiaries made a marked contribution to Soviet foreign policy, not only in the general mobilization of public opinion, but in such specifics as contributing to the anti-war sentiments which led to occasional interference with shipments of war materials to Korea, and, in France, occasioned that turmoil and dissent which surrounded the North Atlantic Alliance during its early years.

By the mid-fifties, however, the peace campaign had fallen into decay, and it all but disintegrated. The unrestrained invective characteristic of Stalinist propaganda strained the credulity, and it soon become obvious to all but the most ardent adepts of the movement that the propaganda was not, in fact, disinterestedly working for peace, but instead was promoting that particular form of peace which the USSR advocated. As a result, the peace campaign entered a credibility crisis, and its sphere of influence contracted almost to the vanishing point. In 1950 the World Peace Council's headquarters were expelled from Paris on grounds of its political one-sidedness, and it moved to Vienna. No sooner was Austrian independence ratified than it was expelled from Vienna in 1955, and thereafter the organization had no stable head-quarters address, but mailed its publications from the address of the International Institute for Peace at its former address in Vienna (and, when questioned, that organization disclaimed any connection with the World Peace Council).

The major reason for the movement's collapse, in addition to the credibility problem, was the end of the Korean War. Once a truce had been achieved the clouds of war seemed to have receded, and in the public mind, subject to an immense range of competing interests in a world of intensive communications, attention to the problems of peace and war was supplanted by other concerns. Because of the general loss of interest in its subject, the peace campaign went into the doldrums, and it would not resume its former significance until a new conflict would arise, again raising the threat of general war to a position of prominent attention.

The peace campaign continued its frequent meetings thereafter, and the Russian Church maintained its habitual participation. But the pro-paganda was ineffective, and it was obvious that the services of the Church in this area were of minimal utility to the interests of Soviet foreign policy in the post-Stalin period.

With the rise of Khrushchev, Soviet foreign policy experienced a radical transformation. While the limitations of the world's political geography remained largely unmodified, with the world polarized be-tween two dominant powers, the Soviet approach to foreign affairs was changed and reformed, inaugurating a new and vastly more complex situation in international political life. The expansion of Soviet foreign policy interests created an immense new field of service in which the Churches might operate in concert with the State.

The fundamental change in Soviet foreign policy was the country's transformation from a continental to a global power. Prior to the death of Stalin, the regime's expansionist appetites had been expressed in expanding the physical borders of the area of Soviet dominance into immediately adjacent areas. The Korean War was no exception to this rule; before the development of the Sino-Soviet dispute, Soviet influence extended through China to North Korea, and the attempt to acquire South Korea as well was consonant with Stalin's general policy of contiguous expansion. No considerable efforts were made to take advantage of possible opportunities where geographic impediments intervened (as, for example, in the Huk uprising in the Philippines) or where unfriendly territories would have to be crossed to gain easy access (as in the case of the post-war turmoil in Burma).

After Stalin's death, however, the new leadership initiated a programme of expanded interest in international affairs which in a comparatively short time would transform the USSR into a global power, able to challenge its major adversary, the US, in any part of the world. Soviet foreign policy began to seek opportunities wherever they might be found. The capabilities of the foreign policy apparatus were modified and augmented accordingly, and the State concurrently undertook a long-range programme of acquisition of the logistical capabilities (primarily air and sea power) necessary to such operations.

This transformation of Soviet foreign policy effected a major expansion in the Church's ability to perform useful services in the interests of the State. If the experience of the later forties had indicated that the policy of contiguous expansion left the Church with only a restricted field of activity, the new policy opened up immense opportunities, for where societies were in turmoil the Church could contribute to Soviet attempts to capitalize on the unrest by the degree to which religion was influential in the country in question.

Khrushchev's revision of the ideological schema for viewing the world also increased the Church's sphere of possible operations. Under Stalin, the world had been viewed in classical terms, as consisting of two hostile camps. The portion of the world under direct Soviet influence constituted the socialist sphere, while all non-socialist (or, more accurately, non-Soviet) areas were in the capitalist camp. In such conditions, in which a black-and-white division was imposed on the world, there was no middle ground, and the Church was limited to working with representatives of the socialist camp and what few overt fellow-travellers could be found within the capitalist sector. This restriction was evident in the peace campaign, for the Church, limited to influencing the small number of outspokenly radical churchmen who collaborated with the World Peace Council (as, for example, the Dean of Canterbury, Hewlett Johnson), had little impact on the Western Churches at large.

Khrushchev modified this approach by postulating a 'Zone of Peace' between the socialist and capitalist camps. The immediate context of the new division was the formerly colonial area of the Third World, where individual countries, while by no means embracing Marxist socialism, nevertheless sought escape from total domination by the capitalist world. By working with such transitional societies, the socialist countries could hope to facilitate their eventual transition to Communism, and hence the USSR had every right and duty to seek all possible effective relations of diplomacy, trade, aid, and influence in this part of the world. The Church, of course, would be able to render some small services to this effort.

There were larger implications, however. By admitting the permissibility of relations with non-socialists, the State freed its foreign policy from the restrictions of working only with Western Communists and their fellow-travellers. Thus the Church could expand the range of its contacts with Western churchmen, seeking not just the outspoken radicals, as before, but exploring all possibilities of gaining any form of co-operation from the Western Churches, regardless of whether or not they were willing to accept the basic tenets of Soviet policy. In view of the kaleidoscopic array of Western Christians, with many individuals and groups having a long tradition of progressive attitudes towards society, this exposed a vast and fertile field for exploration by the Church, which could hope to make effective use of the strong themes of social justice, derived in large measure from the Judaeo-Christian heritage, which were available in the theoretical bases of Marxism.

A new dimension of subtlety also entered the picture with the transformation of Soviet foreign policy. Under Stalin, Soviet policy, particularly in its propaganda aspects, had pursued a totalistic approach, insisting on absolute, unmitigated praise of every aspect of the USSR and its policies. Criticism was to be avoided at all times, and, if necessary, suppressed. With the rise of Khrushchev, this totalistic approach was abandoned in favour of a pragmatic approach, more or less corresponding to the ' small profit margin ' concept in industry. Specific operations were designed to accomplish a specific, limited purpose. Rather than insisting on absolute, unqualified approval of the Soviet Union, an unrealistic design at best, which severely limited the accomplishments of any given operation, the new policy allowed for a broad range of activities, discussions and even criticism, provided only that the specific purpose (e.g. condemnation of German rearmament, or acceptance of Soviet military influence) was accomplished.

This new approach was ideally suited to the capacities of the Church, for it enabled participation in a vast array of activities, where any number of subjects (such as theology, ecumenical relations, etc.) which the State considered irrelevant could be discussed, and in the process the Church could seek to gain approval of the specific, limited points which were of interest to Soviet foreign policy. Nor was the Church subject, as before, to the embarrassment of having to support every aspect of Soviet policy. Inconvenient or uncomfortable considerations, provided they were not germane to the specific result desired, could be avoided, and, if necessary, a degree of criticism of the USSR could be tolerated.

Finally, the new approach of Khrushchev demonstrated a much greater awareness of the importance of public opinion to the successful implementation of Soviet foreign policy. The sarcasm of Stalin's (possibly apocryphal) comment, ' How many divisions has the Pope? ' was subordinated to a realistic appraisal of the need for building a favourable image for the USSR. In this regard, the Church provided the State with one of its most valuable and effective instruments for overcoming the tarnished image of Stalinist Russia in the world outside.

Thus the transformation of Soviet foreign policy after the death of Stalin provided the Church with a broad range of opportunities to render service. The religious dimension of Soviet foreign activities was promoted from a marginal operation on the far fringes of the State's activities to a very important, if still subsidiary, field of action contributing to the over-all realization of Soviet designs in international affairs.

4   The Christian Peace Conference

THE most spectacular and successful example of the expanded role of religion in Soviet foreign policy was the Prague Christian Peace Conference.[1] A new experiment, the CPC—although without precedent in the history of the Church's international activities—drew heavily on the experience of similar formations in other areas of Soviet foreign policy, and was a carefully devised, intelligently constructed, highly organized endeavour which returned handsome dividends in furthering the interests of the USSR in the modern world.

The public history of the formation of the CPC gives evidence of meticulous preparation, and, indeed, a considerable period elapsed between the first initiatives and the appearance of the CPC as a fully formed, functioning organization. According to a Czech Protestant publication, professors of the Comenius Theological Faculty in Prague met colleagues from the Lutheran Church in Slovakia in October 1957, and the suggestion was raised that an international conference be held to clarify the Christian position on atomic weapons.[2] In December the Ecumenical Council of Churches of Czechoslovakia decided to hold a Christian Peace Conference in 1958, which was attended by some 40 delegates from Eastern Europe and West Germany. A Standing Committee of 17 members was formed. A similar meeting was held the following year, with 70 participants. At the third conference, in 1960, there were 120 delegates, and four working groups were formed. Messages were sent to the World Council of Churches, heads of government of the four great powers, the United Nations, and all Christians in general. At this meeting plans were ratified for the convocation of an All Christian Peace Assembly (ACPA) in Prague the following year.

With the First ACPA, the CPC was fully formed and operational. Seven hundred delegates were attracted to the Assembly, and during the meeting (13–18 June 1961) officers were elected, a fairly elaborate organizational structure was ratified, and a number of subsidiary units and national affiliates were established. A vigorous programme of activity was initiated, and thereafter meetings of larger or smaller units of the CPC took place frequently in widely scattered locations. The movement grew rapidly. At the Second ACPA in Prague in 1964, nearly 1,000 attended, including official or unofficial observers from many international and national religious and denominational bodies, and more than 50 representatives of the working press. For the next three years the CPC engaged in vigorous activities, attracting maximum publicity on a wide variety of issues, and holding meetings with great frequency in numerous locations throughout the world.

The movement's climax came in March 1968, when the Third ACPA was convened in Prague. It was attended by some 660 people, and the movement, by now a mature organization, well founded and with a firm base established in several countries, including the US, could speak with assurance, particularly on those special issues which were of prime importance to its interests. In addition, because of the rampant liberalization then going forward in Czechoslovakia, the proceedings were lively and debate was vigorous, and many of the delegates who had arrived with certain reservations were persuaded in the course of the ACPA of the validity and value of the movement.

The Prague Christian Peace Conference was admirably equipped for facilitating Soviet foreign policy. Its primary function in this regard was to contribute to the revitalization of propaganda for peace as an adjunct to the implementation of Soviet interests. As has been noted, the peace movement was isolated and inconsequential after the middle fifties. Under Khrushchev, a serious—and ultimately—successful effort was undertaken to refurbish the movement. In the continuing confrontation of two major centres of world power, the peace theme remained potentially important, and Soviet foreign policy would be weakened without this adjunct to its operations. Attempts were made to break out of the impasse which had been created by the unsubtle machinations of the World Peace Council under Stalin, and the CPC was one of the most effective and spectacular successes in a redesigned and expanded mobilization of peace propaganda in Soviet foreign policy.

A more immediate service which the CPC could perform was to act as a counter-weight to certain other operations which were under consideration at the time. In the less rigid environment of Soviet foreign affairs, the Church in the East was being allowed to give up the adamant hostility to Western Churches which had been characteristic of the earlier period. The ecumenical movement was being reconsidered, not so much in the older terms of representing a threat to Soviet interests, but rather as an opportunity, and in the later fifties negotiations were in train which would lead to the admission of the Russian Orthodox Church to membership of the World Council of Churches in 1961. Particularly to the authorities of the Soviet State, the World Council was something of an unknown quantity, and although it was obvious that potential benefits might be gained from Russian Church participation, there was no clear understanding of what risks might be involved. The creation of the CPC could serve as a form of insurance, providing a mechanism which could be utilized if participation in the World Council proved harmful.

Particularly during the early years of Russian participation in the ecumenical movement, considerable effort was devoted to portraying the CPC as a competitor of the well-established World Council of Churches. In 1962 Patriarch Aleksii said of the CPC, 'As we all know, there is no other Christian movement or organization at the present time that fully expresses the efforts of ordinary Christians in the East or the West to help effect the reconciliation of mankind.' [3] The journal of the CPC carried frequent statements of this nature:

> The Christian Peace Conference is today the only bridge between East and West; it stands completely outside the explicitly political sphere and attempts to seek a solution for peaceful co-existence from a Christian standpoint.[4]
>
> Undoubtedly one of the factors in the initiative that led to the Prague movement is the circumstance that in certain experiences with the Oekumene [ecumenical movement] something was lacking. Whereas the Oekumene was an appeal against self-sufficiency and isolationist tendencies of different churches, the Prague movement developed a critical function in regard to the Oekumene, in the best and healthiest sense of criticism—a challenge. This was how it was understood in Geneva. At first, of course, it aroused two reactions of opposition: Prague was regarded with suspicion as an ' Eastern Oekumene '. . .[5]
>
> I emphasize—so that there may be no doubt of this point—that these different conferences are not a duplication of the work of the World Council of Churches, for two reasons: they afford a broader platform (e.g., in contacts with Chinese churches); they facilitate the meeting of a larger number of church members and endeavor—especially through the regional conferences—to get concretely down to the congregational level.[6]

Thus the CPC represented itself as an equal, if not a superior, of the World Council, and, should participation in the latter prove harmful to the interests of Soviet foreign policy, the Russian Churches could be persuaded to retreat to a second organization better able to accomplish the desired functions.

With the passage of time, Russian participation in the World Council of Churches did not prove nearly so inimical to Soviet interests as the State may have feared (indeed, in one of the curious ironies of history, it was participation in the CPC, not the World Council, which ultimately presented a serious threat to Soviet interests, as will become apparent below). Hence, after the Second ACPA in 1964, this competitive theme disappeared from the CPC literature, and in its place harmonious relations with the ecumenical movement were enthusiastically sought.

A third major function of the CPC in the portfolio of Soviet foreign policy was to contribute to the extension of Soviet influence in the non-aligned world. High priority was placed on this endeavour, and in large measure the CPC was oriented to the Third World rather than to the East-West confrontation. Great efforts were expended on attracting members from the under-developed nations, with much more time, travel and, ultimately, representation devoted to the Third World than to the West. Indeed, to a degree, the CPC may have been motivated in its sometimes desultory attempts to gain adherents in the West by this prior interest. Because of the missionary and imperial tradition, many of the Churches in the Third World looked to the Western parent Churches for guidance, and even token participation by the West in the CPC might yield considerable benefits in establishing the organization's credentials, thereby encouraging Christians from the Third World to participate.

A number of general approaches were utilized by the CPC which are characteristic of the transformed Soviet foreign policy of the post-Stalin era. Perhaps most obvious is the employment of an allied country to initiate the project, rather than reliance on direct Soviet leadership. While the Russian Churches played an important part in the movement, the CPC itself was originated and presided over by Czech churchmen. In this regard, the CPC conformed to a pattern applied in many other areas of Soviet foreign policy, in which an Eastern European country played a leading role, while the Soviet Union was content to remain in the background.

One of the chief reasons for the success of the CPC was adherence to the limited-achievement policy of operation. Participating churchmen were free, and, indeed, encouraged to discuss a broad range of topics which, whether or not they were ultimately related to the theme of peace, were irrelevant to the interests of Soviet foreign policy. The resulting atmosphere of unrestricted dialogue and theological interchange was highly attractive to many of the movement's participants who otherwise might not be especially convinced of the validity of certain of the more sharply pointed resolutions. Accepting such resolutions on a relatively small number of highly political themes seemed a small price to pay in order to achieve the benefits of the broader dialogue on subjects which, if subsidiary to the interests of the USSR, were of chief interest for such delegates. As a result, a much broader circle of churchmen, with a correspondingly greater degree of influence in the non-Soviet world, contributed to the work of the CPC than the earlier forms of the peace movement had ever been able to attract.

The chief tactic employed by the CPC in accomplishing its ends was in defining the issue of peace. In this regard, Khrushchev's emphasis on, and reinterpretation of, the term 'peaceful coexistence', was of great benefit in the work of the CPC. In its discussions, the CPC from its inception structured the topic of peace in the terms of this concept, and over a period of time was able successfully to narrow the options to this concept alone as an alternative to war. Other approaches to avoidance of war were ignored, or, if necessary, allowed to be raised and then absorbed without altering the conclusions reached.

'Peaceful coexistence' in Soviet parlance was never defined or given a detailed content, and this was one of its great virtues in the practice of Soviet foreign policy. By no means did the concept categorically deny the use of armed force. 'Wars of national liberation' and violent revolution against colonial or neo-colonial oppression were fully legitimate, and while attempts to suppress any such conflicts were defined as aggression, massive aid could be given to the rebelling side in the conflict without violation of 'peaceful coexistence' between the two social systems. Basically, the term only implied avoidance of major war between the two opposing forces in the world, or, in other circumstances, avoidance of major war involving weapons of mass destruction, or even, perhaps, major war initiated by the West against the East. All other forms of competition, including very vigorous ones, were permissible under the concept, and, indeed, major attempts to upset the atomic balance of power, as in the Cuban crisis, could be undertaken by the USSR without violating 'peaceful coexistence' (although resisting such attempts did constitute a violation).

By narrowing the alternatives to war to 'peaceful coexistence', the CPC was able effectively to channel sentiments against war into forms which were of direct applicability to Soviet foreign policy. Once this definition of peace was accepted, to refrain from supporting Soviet actions became very difficult indeed, and on occasion the terminology used in the CPC allowed application of the resolutions and recommendations in the context of general Soviet policy in ways which might not be foreseen by some of CPC's participants.

Unlike earlier participation of the Church in the peace movement, the CPC made no secret of the fact that its purposes were political. Under Stalin, Church participants in the meetings of the World Peace Council and other agencies claimed to stand above politics, carefully and repeatedly denying any involvement whatsoever in the political issues of the day. The CPC did not emulate this dubious procedure, which was scarcely credible in any event, but openly and avowedly admitted to involvement in political action, sanctified by Christianity perhaps, but political nonetheless. According to the CPC journal:

I. We must not try to escape from the tension inherent in our theme: politics is one of the most fundamental and vital functions of a secularized world ... Politics is the sphere where secularization becomes most apparent and where at the same time Jesus Christ reigns.

II. If Christians wish to serve as conciliators in the sphere of politics, they must first be reconciled to politics, that is, they must cease considering it an image which must be respected, or avoiding it as if [it] were taboo. Only by secularizing the taboo of politics can we gain a correct view of the meaning of politics, its necessity and its relativity regarding a realistic figure of man. All else is a perversion of politics.

III. The service of reconciliation in politics means not allowing the past to overwhelm you, but taking it over in a penitent posture which liberates us from any sort of self-righteousness.[7]

Above all, we must not speak here of politics without knowing the true aspect of politics, which is a never relaxed tension, it is a confrontation, a test of force, a struggle with varying results to take power ... where restriction is necessary to suppress disorder, where the strongest hold sway, where both one side and the other are opposed, in order that their own interests should win out.[8]

A second [unacceptable Christian approach] is a mere moralistic protestation against our own society—with the consequence that in such a case Christians are deprived more and more of contacts with the society in which they live and thus are pushed farther and farther into internal isolation ... This all occurs in the effort to avoid acting in a political way, even though the results of such behavior are markedly political, and in a negative sense of the word.[9]

One of the chief advantages which the CPC possessed was a well developed theological rationale, which allowed a peculiar congruency between CPC interests and those of Soviet foreign policy. The CPC was able to provide an independent foundation for its advocacy of peace, based on a theological approach, which freed it from the burdensome necessity of attempting to justify—or even consider—the ideological structure utilized by Soviet theoreticians in support of the international policies of the USSR. In large measure, this theological rationale was the work of the founder and President of the CPC, Joseph L. Hromadka.[10] A creative theologian in his own right, Hromadka had spent the Nazi period at Princeton Theological Seminary in the US and after the war had returned to his native Czechoslovakia. For the two following decades he enjoyed an increasing international reputation for his theological formulae, providing a Christian approach to the conduct of Church affairs in a society led by the Communist Party. Hromadka's theology provided the basic approach for the work of the CPC, and, indeed, it is doubtful whether the CPC could have arisen without his services.

A number of aspects of this theological platform were suited to devising an approach to the problems of peace and war which could coexist harmoniously with the interests of Soviet foreign policy. The primary theme of the theology was a pervasive, almost exclusive emphasis on the social implications of the Christian faith. Social justice, equality, and the brotherhood of all men under the common fatherhood of God were ubiquitous themes. In particular, the many and obvious instances of injustice and exploitation of man by man in the capitalist tradition were seized upon, and, with little attention to possible balancing virtues of the system, capitalism was rather uncritically denounced as evil, in need of replacement if the Christian commitment to social justice were to be realized. Conversely, the lofty goals of Marxism, promising the final elimination from society of evil and exploitation, were accepted with little critical analysis of any untoward effects which might vitiate these aspirations in contemporary practice. The result amounted to a theological equation of socialism and capitalism with good and evil, respectively.

A second theme of the theology, traceable, perhaps, to the traumas of World War II, was the doctrine of collective guilt. In view of the homogeneity of complex, modern society, all men share in the guilt of, and responsibility for, evil in the community of man. It would be simplistic to pretend that evil does not exist; but it would be irresponsible to blame others when, in fact, the Christian must recognize his own guilt for what has happened in his global society. This subtle formulation permitted recognition of certain of the unpleasant realities of contemporary Soviet actions without allowing hostility against the

USSR to develop, for the Christian acknowledges, first and foremost, his own guilt in the total situation.

It is certain, in this context, that the primitive anti-communism of most of the western countries (the public mentality, the press, the government speeches), the revival in the German Federal Republic of a certain number of military or judicial personages who played a very definite role in the last war, the placing of American bases at the frontiers of the USSR, can only confirm that country in the conviction that it is encircled and this must necessarily flavour, in consequence, the action of those who are more strongly partisan to a hard policy, even envisaging the eventuality of a third world conflict. I am saying all this because I am speaking to the West. With my Soviet friends I have used a quite different language as you may imagine. I am not giving here any value judgment: what counts is not to say yes or no, whether the USSR is right, but to know what reactions are brought about by one attitude or another on our part.[11]

The theological formulations of the CPC laid great emphasis on the infinite value of human life. The concept that life categorically supersedes all other values, which is simple, obvious fact from a secular point of view (life being the prerequisite for the achievement of any values whatsoever), represents something of a novelty in the Christian tradition, with its strong themes of sacrifice and the subordination of temporal values to the eternal. Once absolute value had been attributed to human life, however, the duty to avoid war at all costs was an obvious corollary, for no possible subsidiary ideals could justify accepting death or inflicting it on others.

Because human life was elevated to predominance in the hierarchy of value, the doctrine of the just war all but dropped from sight. Scriptural passages extolling the sanctity of human life were heavily emphasized, and little or no attention was paid to alternate passages which might be utilized in support of justifiable warfare in certain circumstances. Because war necessarily involves taking of life, it is by definition evil and impermissible for the Christian. (In this regard, however, a certain ambivalence should be noted. The fundamental emphasis on social justice might perhaps come into conflict with the dogma of the sanctity of human life, and where violence is utilized to overcome social injustice, as in ' wars of national liberation ' or violent revolutions, taking of life might be justifiable as an unavoidable necessity to the achievement of social justice.)

In its specific concerns, the war in Vietnam was of overwhelming importance to the CPC. As had been the case in the Korean War, the existence of a fully organized, functioning facility for encouragement of anti-war sentiments well before the war had assumed serious proportions was immensely fortunate for Soviet foreign policy. Conversely, much of the success of the CPC may be attributed to the increased apprehension throughout the world occasioned by the rise of a serious local war which threatened escalation into a world conflict of unthinkable consequences. The doldrums of the post-Korean peace campaign were reversed by Vietnam, and the Khrushchev regime, already committed to a revitalization of the peace propaganda, was in a position to capitalize on the return of the issue to first place in the public mind.

The CPC's treatment of the Vietnam conflict was a constant, long-term, patiently waged, and ultimately, highly successful struggle. Well before such formulations became fashionable in the West, the conflict was referred to in uncompromising terms of outside aggression, in collusion with a dictatorial South Vietnamese regime, unlawfully and immorally attempting to suppress the true representatives of the Vietnamese people themselves. Over the long term, this interpretative schema became accepted, if only by default, in the CPC, which was able to buttress its argument by attracting token representation of the National Liberation Front to its meetings from time to time. Messages and resolutions were sent to governments, intergovernmental agencies, religious organizations, and Christians and all men of good will, frequently and in great abundance, protesting against American actions in Vietnam in the strongest of terms.

Perhaps more important, the CPC, because it was already mobilized to the issue, was able to present a coherent, understandable formula for approaching the Vietnamese problem, with highly developed and immensely detailed analyses from Biblical, theological, sociological, political, and other points of view. As public apprehension developed, and, particularly in the Western Churches, the conviction spread that something must be done to halt the carnage, the formulations of the CPC were available to provide specific content and a detailed programme to answer the vague and still formless quest within the Churches for some answer to the problem of Vietnam. In large measure, the growing concern within the Churches ultimately found expression in terms which had already been worked out by the CPC, and the resulting wave of revulsion against the war thus took a form which was more compatible with the interests of Soviet foreign policy than might have been the case otherwise.

It should not be supposed, however, that the CPC—or Soviet propaganda in general—was primarily responsible for the massive public hostility to the war. A great many factors were involved, and the Vietnamese war, in view of its ambiguity, complexity, cost in human lives, and indecisive results, and especially in view of the confusion reigning because of rapidly changing social structures and the transformation of traditional values throughout the world, doubtless would have engendered massive revulsion with or without the machinations of Soviet propaganda. At the same time, it should be noted that particularly in the US the Churches played a significant role in the process of elevating hostility to the war to a powerful, indeed overwhelming, protest throughout the society. To the degree that the CPC was successful in assisting the Churches in this regard, it must share at least a portion of the credit for the generation of the great wave of revulsion in the US and throughout the world which, ultimately, was chiefly responsible for frustrating the original designs of American military involvement in Vietnam.

Vietnam was not the sole concern of the CPC, of course. A broad range of issues appeared in the work of the CPC, and a concert of allied projects was undertaken. Of particular interest was the attempt to influence the workings of the World Council of Churches. From its very inception, and particularly after the Russian Churches had become integrated into the structure of the ecumenical movement, the CPC devoted much effort to influencing it. Despite the advice of World Council leaders, the CPC was careful to hold both its First and Third All Christian Peace assemblies immediately prior to the important assemblies of the World Council in 1961 and 1968. Great publicity was given to the participation of the World Council in the meetings of the CPC, even if only to the extent of sending observers or in the person of CPC members who also were or had been World Council officers. CPC desires to have its views reflected in the ecumenical movement were not completely frustrated. On a number of issues—particularly on the question of violent revolution—positions taken by the World Council were not altogether dissimilar to the approaches advocated by the CPC.

In its approach to the problems of the Third World, the CPC was able to provide a coherent rationale from the point of view of a Christian theology. In line with its social doctrine, the CPC considered colonialism and capitalist imperialism conducive to social evil, and hence the Christian is in duty bound to support the replacement of such structures. Consistent with the formulations of Soviet ideology under Khrushchev, this antipathy to colonialism was extended to include neo-colonialism, or the continuation of the system by economic, social, or other pressures and influences after political independence had been achieved.

The CPC placed great emphasis on the problem of poverty as illustrative of this general theme. Much effort was devoted to the analyses and elucidation of the prevailing economic imbalance between the advanced and the under-developed countries, and numerous resolutions and appeals were produced demanding radically increased governmental aid, primarily from the developed countries of the West, to the impoverished Third World.

Of particular importance was the doctrine of revolution. The pressing need for eradication of social injustice made it imperative for the Christian to advocate immediate and sweeping change of the entire structure of society in the colonial and neo-colonial world. Evolution, or processes of gradual change within the existing social structure, received scant attention in the deliberations of the CPC; what was needed was revolution. And despite the apparent incongruity with CPC formulations regarding peace and war, the need for reform is so pressing that the Christian cannot but give unqualified support to violent revolution in such cases, for anything short of that is doomed to failure. Violence can be condoned, and indeed advocated, for otherwise the just demands of those peoples who have long been subject to unconscionable discrimination present the gravest of threats to world peace and security.

The structure of the CPC was admirably designed, giving every appearance of control by popular democracy without sacrificing sufficient organizational command to permit highly efficient operation.[12] In actual fact, the CPC was much less responsive to the will of its general constituency than its structure might indicate at first glance.

According to the Statute of the CPC, the periodic All Christian Peace Assembly is the source of all authority in the organization, and its decision, expressed by majority vote, is binding. However, there are certain anomalies in the Statute which modify this formula somewhat. Membership in the ACPA consists of ' all churches, groups, and individuals agreeing with the principle and mission of the movement '. No provision is made for any scheme of weighted voting, and hence Churches and groups represented by delegations have no promise that the proceedings will accurately reflect the views of the larger constituency they represent. Furthermore, the inclusion of individuals, with no other qualifications than agreement with the movement's principle and mission, offers no guarantee that the ACPA will not reflect primarily the desires of delegates from the host country. Even in the absence of political pressures (official encouragement of large participation by local citizens, visa restrictions for foreign delegates, etc.) the costs and difficulties of distance make some imbalance inevitable in a movement which claims to represent a world-wide constituency.

The actual implementation of the authority of the ACPA is limited to electing the movement's President and General Secretary, and the members of the Working Committee and Advisory Committee. No other forms of control are provided by the Statute, and the ACPA has no specific authority for recall or impeachment of elected or appointed officials, veto or revision of actions taken by other organs of the CPC, review or disapproval of financial transactions, or establishment of agendas and priorities for any CPC functions, including the deliberations of the ACPA itself.

According to the Statute, ' The Working Committee, headed by the President of the movement, is the directing body of the CPC in the period between the meetings of the ACPA.' Actual authority is located in this body, which until 1964 consisted of 16 members, 9 from the USSR and Eastern Europe, and then was expanded to 25 members, 13 from non-socialist countries (6 Western and 7 Third World). All decisions are by simple majority. The Working Committee elects all members and officers of the organization not elected by the ACPA.

Between sessions of the Working Committee, the business of the CPC is transacted by an even smaller body, the International Secretariat, elected by the Working Committee and led by the Secretary-General. Inasmuch as no limitations are placed by the Statute on the International Secretariat's transaction of business, and particularly in view of the fact that ' it also prepares the agenda of the elected bodies and represents the movement in accordance with the principles and aims of the CPC ', it would seem that actual control of the movement is vested in this very small group of officers, modified somewhat by such control as is exercised by the Working Committee when it is in session.

No mechanisms are given by the Statute for control of the actions of these bodies. There is no provision for abrogation, reversal, amendment or modification of actions, decisions or statements of the International Secretariat by the Working Committee, of either group by the ACPA, or of individual officers by any organ of the CPC. Furthermore, according to the ' Order of business of the CPC ', the Working Committee formulates the agenda for the ACPA, and ' only such points that are in the agenda can be discussed '.[13]

The financial operations of the CPC are delegated to the Financial Commission, with eight members appointed by the Working Committee. Financial disbursements are the sole responsibility of the President and General Secretary of the CPC (both elected by the ACPA) and the Chairman and Secretary of the Financial Commission (elected by the Working Committee), the signatures of any two required for disbursement of funds. The proceedings of the Financial Commission are subject to only nominal control. It 'prepares the annual budget and submits it to the Working Committee for approval', but no provisions are made for amending or revising the budget. Annual accounts are submitted to the Advisory Committee (see below), but no powers, not even that of approval, are specifically given to the latter with regard to this annual accounting. There is no other provision in the Statute for audit and control of the movement's financial transactions.

Thus it would appear that the CPC, despite appearances of democratic control in the ACPA, is able to function as a tightly disciplined organization controlled by a simple majority of the small group of leaders comprising the Working Committee, or even by a majority of the even smaller International Secretariat.

Other organs of the CPC structure are given no role in the control of the organization. No limitations are mentioned in the Statute regarding the ability of the officers, particularly the President and the General Secretary, to speak in the name of the entire CPC. The Advisory Committee for Continuation of the Work of the CPC is a large, unwieldy organization of well over 100 members elected by the Working Committee. It meets annually at least, and its function is limited to an advisory capacity. Its major role in the operations of the CPC has been to provide an additional means of publicizing the movement's views. Standing Commissions, usually about a dozen, are also elected by the Working Committee to meet periodically and consider, discuss and provide advice and counsel on their particular concerns (' Peace and Freedom ', ' Peace and the Cold War ', ' Peace and the New States ', ' Peace and the German Question ', ' Misuse of Christianity ', etc.).

In addition, the CPC established a number of Regional Committees to augment the work of the central organization. The most influential of these, outside Eastern Europe and the USSR, was the German Regional Committee, with perhaps 400 members in the Federal Republic. Some of these Regional Committees were able to produce a certain amount of additional publicity favourable to the interests of the CPC; others, such as those of Switzerland and Great Britain, were eminently ineffective, while the Regional Committee of India appeared to exist in name only.   After the 1964 ACPA it became possible to establish a very promising United States Committee for the Christian Peace Conference, with the respected theologian from Princeton, Charles C. West, as Chairman, and Kurtis F. Naylor, Associate Secretary of the prestigious National Council of Churches' Department of International Affairs, as Executive Secretary.

It is difficult to assess the scope and size of the activities of the CPC. Financial reports, normally a convenient index to the magnitude of an organization's operations, have not been made public by the CPC. In 1961 the CPC budget was estimated to be approximately $130,000. In 1962 it was announced that the organization's budget would be doubled for the following year. An ACPA, of which there have been three, costs an estimated $1,000,000. In view of the costs involved in maintaining current operations and staff, publishing (the CPC issues its illustrated, bi-monthly journal in three languages as well as illustrated booklets and mimeographed bulletins at frequent intervals), and travel by officers and members of the CPC, the operation has required a considerable investment of resources.

According to the CPC, all funds come from the members of the movement, but little information is available concerning the distribution of the financial burden. In the 1961 budget, $110,000 (80 per cent) was said to come from Eastern European and Soviet members and member Churches. Some verification of the level of expenditures of the CPC can be made deductively. Taking 1965 as a more or less typical year, the CPC indicated specific attendance for nine of its various meetings (three in Prague; two in Moscow, and one each at Budapest; Freetown, Sierra Leone; Halle, German Democratic Republic; and in Austria). Computation of the air fares (round trip, economy jet) for the participants in this portion of the CPC's activities in 1965 yields a minimum of $54,393.20 expended on transportation, over and above other travel, accommodation, publications, and on-going expenses (office, staff, overheads) of the CPC. In 1965 the Regional Committee in West Germany, by far the most active and vigorous of the CPC's affiliates in the West, made a total contribution of DM 3,000 ($750) to the CPC. Hence it would seem a reasonable assumption that the bulk of the movement's financial resources come from Eastern Europe and the USSR.

The CPC was an intelligently devised instrument for the propagation of a particular approach to the subject of peace, broad and flexible in its range of subjects, efficient and well controlled in its organization, and with every appearance of legitimacy. Any Soviet control which might have existed was deeply sublimated—to the extent that such control could only be inferred—and at no time was it prominent or visibly displayed. With such advantages, the CPC was remarkably successful, able to render significant service to Soviet foreign policy without appearing to be tied to one single point of view on all subjects and at all times. Unfortunately, it was these very advantages which contained in them the seeds of the movement's collapse, and its virtual elimination as an adjunct to Soviet foreign policy.

Centrifugal forces in Eastern Europe grew to immense proportions during the sixties, and at the beginning of 1968, after the fall of Novotny, a serious situation began to develop in Czechoslovakia. The country entered on its brief experiment in liberalization, culminating in the invasion of Prague by Warsaw Pact forces on 21 August 1968. The invasion marked the beginning of the swift decline, and, as it would appear, eventual collapse of the CPC.

It was precisely those devices which had been intelligently built into the CPC, ensuring the organization's success in the peace movement, which contributed to its eventual failure as an auxiliary of Soviet foreign policy. The basic strategy employed by the USSR of allowing one of its allied countries to take the leading role in a particular aspect of international relations, while the Soviet Union contented itself with a less visible role in the background, was premised on the assumption that sufficient congruence would exist between the policies of the USSR and the allied country in question. When the diminution of Soviet control in Eastern Europe resulted in a radical divergence between Soviet and Czechoslovak interests, this mechanism of indirect control was no longer viable, and organizations such as the CPC, under Czech, rather than Soviet, leadership, would no longer function in a manner completely satisfactory to Soviet interests.

Furthermore, the vagueness of the structural rules of the CPC also contributed to a diminished degree of control in the new situation in 1968. If such imprecision in the Statute was designed to permit strict guidance and direction of the organization's activities according to a preconceived format, it also carried the unforeseen possibility of allowing the leaders to guide the activity in other directions should they desire. With the radical decrease in Soviet control in Czechoslovakia, the structure of the CPC left Soviet representatives with no means of direct control over the movement's predominantly Czech leaders.

Finally, even the practice of limited achievement in the CPC's meetings, whereby participants were encouraged to express themselves on any number of subsidiary issues provided they adhered to the desired policy on the small number of decisive matters, contributed to the movement's demise. This subtle approach made a signal contribution to the CPC's ability to attract an impressive circle of adherents; it simply would not work, however, once the leaders themselves began to be more interested in the subsidiary issues than in the matters which were considered crucial by the USSR. In the heady atmosphere of Prague in 1968, the Third ACPA was the scene of very animated discussions indeed, and certain of the desired resolutions were passed only with the greatest difficulty.

The CPC had responded with great caution to the liberalization movement.[14] However, the invasion of Prague elicited an instant and outspoken reaction. On 22 August Hromadka wrote an open letter to the Soviet Ambassador expressing his dismay:

The bond of friendship between Czechoslovakia and the Soviet Union has been destroyed. The danger exists that our people's love will turn to hatred and that our nearest friends will appear as our enemies.

The Soviet government could not have committed a more tragic error. It is an immeasurable misfortune. The moral weight of socialism and communism has been shattered for a long time to come.[15]

Earlier, the International Secretariat of the CPC had issued a vigorous protest against the invasion. This protest drew a strong reaction from the Russian Orthodox Church on 14 September:

Dear Dr. Hromadka, we have just received the press bulletin of the World Council of Churches, No. 31, of 29 August 1968, in which, citing the German Evangelical Press Service, we read of a sharp protest ' against the illegal invasion of Soviet and other Eastern European forces in Czechoslovakia,' which the ' Secretariat of the Prague Christian Peace Conference ' allegedly issued on 21 August. According to the data we have in hand, this statement was made in Prague by two workers of the apparatus of the Christian Peace Conference, who do not have the rights and are not able to represent by their own persons either the Christian Peace Conference as a whole or any organ of the Conference which has the right to make public statements.

This statement already on 22 August of this year was published in Western Germany and received wide dissemination in international Church circles.

Such conduct by co-workers of the apparatus of the CPC demands, in our opinion, condemnation by the leadership of the Conference, for we know that many members of the Christian Peace Conference do not share the point of view of the authors of the aforementioned statement.

In fact, the understanding of 'occupation' which the authors of the statement employ is inapplicable in the present case, when the armies of the five countries allied with the CSSR defended the socialist structure in Czechoslovakia, which was threatened, and accomplished the overthrow of the anti-socialist forces. We are convinced that the temporary introduction of the forces allied with the CSSR on the territory of Czechoslovakia prevented great bloodshed and, possibly, international armed conflict.

We pray for the fraternal people of Socialist Czechoslovakia and for their manifold development.

With unchanged fraternal love for you in Christ,

Aleksii
Patriarch of Moscow and All Russia [16]

Apparently the re-establishment of controls over the CPC occasioned no less difficulty than the Soviet State was experiencing in consolidating political control over Czechoslovakia. Subsequent activities and meetings of CPC organs were filled with tension, and over the next year and a half the organization functioned on a progressively diminished scale. Massive resistance arose within the membership to suggestions that the headquarters of the movement be transferred to Budapest or East Berlin, and the plan was abandoned, at least temporarily.

In July 1969 the Moscow Patriarchate convened an independent Conference of All Religions in Defense of Peace at Zagorsk, near Moscow. *Inter alia*, this event may have been intended as a warning to the CPC, for since the CPC's inception the Russian Church had not normally acted unilaterally in the peace field. Although numerous foreign observers attended, invitations to the luminaries who had been the major contributors to the CPC were conspicuous by their absence. The conference, like its predecessor in 1952, attracted representatives of non-Christian religions of the USSR, thus reaching a broader range of religions than the CPC, Christian by definition, had been able to do. The Zagorsk conference provided an example of the controlled, disciplined approach to the problem of peace, without outbursts or controversies which might be embarrassing to Soviet foreign policy interests. In this regard, the speeches at the conference were much more reminiscent of the peace movement of Stalin's day than of that subtlety which had characterized the CPC.[17]

The final event in the CPC's history as an effective and credible movement came in November 1969, when J. Ondra, the General Secretary, was forced to resign. Hromadka himself immediately tendered his own resignation, on the grounds that Ondra had been unjustly removed by political pressure applied by a small group within the CPC.[18] Hromadka, then eighty-one years old, succumbed to heart failure a few weeks later. With the loss of Hromadka, who more than any other figure had been identified as the father and leader of the CPC, and who possessed independent stature as a creative theologian unique among the active clergy of the Eastern Churches, the movement suffered irreparable damage, and although it has not as yet formally dissolved itself, it seems most unlikely that it will again be able to function with any effectiveness whatsoever in support of Soviet policy, particularly in the non-Soviet world.

5 The Third World

WITH the Soviet Union's transformation into a global power, a concerted effort has been made to extend Soviet influence into the uncommitted world. The US and the USSR are locked in a stalemate of power; although it is still possible, any radical realignment of the industrially developed world seems unlikely, and, in particular, the nuclear stalemate appears unalterable, short of catastrophe, in the foreseeable future. In such circumstances, with a relatively immobile division of power in the developed world, it is the Third World which offers the best prospects for extending the Soviet sphere of influence. Spectacular successes have been achieved in this theatre of operations by means of a foreign policy which is exceedingly diversified. In addition to the more traditional modes of expansion through direct Communist Party influences, a broad range of techniques has been utilized in seeking to expand Soviet influence by diplomatic, economic, and other available means. With the rather belated emphasis on endowing the Soviet military with a flexible-response capability, it would appear that Soviet foreign policy has not yet exhausted its opportunities in the Third World.

Religion has a place in Soviet policy towards the Third World, even though perhaps its role is not so important as in the predominantly Christian, advanced nations. With the exception of Latin America, Christianity embraces only a miniscule fraction of the population of the Third World, and hence, at first glance, the role of the Churches in Soviet foreign policy towards these areas might seem correspondingly small. However, both in Asia and Africa, Christianity plays a more important role in some countries than population percentages might suggest. The great educational efforts of Christian missionary enterprises in these areas have exposed a large percentage of the educated élite to Christian influences, and as a result, the minority Churches in certain countries enjoy a large representation at the centres of governmental, economic, and social power. An added dimension in Asia, Africa, and the Middle East is the impact of Islam and Buddhism in these areas; this will be treated in the next chapter.

In the competition for the Third World, Russian Christianity is at a considerable disadvantage, for it does not share the centuries of intense missionary tradition of the Western countries. But the USSR's ability to make even a restricted use of religion in its foreign policy gives it a signal advantage over the third major competitor for influence, China. The world's religious demography, together with the greater doctrinal (and antireligious) purity of Communist China, precludes its exploitation of religion almost entirely in non-Asiatic sectors of the underdeveloped world.

The major instrument of extension of Soviet influence to the Third World via religion, as has been indicated, was the Prague Christian Peace Conference. The CPC directed its greatest efforts towards attracting and influencing Christians from the Third World, with frequent delegations and various meetings taking place throughout Asia, Africa, and South America. The goals, strategies, and successes of the CPC constitute the major contribution of religion to Soviet Third World policies. The CPC, however, did not exhaust the range of attempts by Soviet and Eastern European Churches to exercise an influence in the Third World, and, in fact, the measures used to add a religious dimension to Soviet influence in these areas were considerably broader than the specific approaches and areas of CPC interest might suggest.

Soviet activities in Africa have been vigorous, but with mixed results. The social and political turmoil have offered much promise for gaining influence, while the extreme poverty and thirst for rapid advancement have provided fertile soil for the USSR, both in regard to the propagation of Communism as a means for rapid industrialization (using Russia as the example) and for the more direct possibilities of trade and aid. However, like all other suitors for African affections, the USSR has experienced great frustration due to the seemingly insoluble problems of political instability which are rife in Africa. Furthermore, vigorous Chinese competition has added to the complexity of African problems for Soviet foreign policy.

The role of the Churches in African affairs has been limited. Ethiopia, with its well-developed Christian tradition, has been the recipient of Russian delegations and exchanges of visits, as have Uganda, Madagascar, and, particularly, Kenya.[1] In 1966 five students from Ethiopia were allowed to enter a four-year course of theological studies in the USSR as guests of the Moscow Patriarchate,[2] while in 1967 a student from Madagascar was pursuing graduate theological studies in Prague.[3] In 1964 the Russian Orthodox Church donated eighty-six cases of laboratory equipment to the National Christian Council of Kenya,[4] and in 1967 the Evangelical Church in Madagascar received a tractor from the Czech Brethren for its agricultural school.[5]

The Churches have played a very cautious role with regard to the various crises on the African continent. The CPC on occasion denounced foreign intervention in the Congo early in the sixties,[6] and in 1968 its Third ACPA produced a resolution deploring the ' balkanization ' of Nigeria.[7] Otherwise the Churches by and large refrained from any intense agitation with regard to the Nigerian Civil War, although in 1969 a delegation of Christians from Nigeria was received by the Moscow Patriarchate.[8] In any case, the Nigerian conflict was a confused situation for religion in Soviet foreign policy, for while the sympathies of the State lay with the Nigerian government, it was the Biafrans who were of predominantly Christian persuasions.

In the general propaganda directed towards Africa religion has played a contributory role. The Churches have joined in the all but universal denunciation of discriminatory racial policies in South Africa and Rhodesia,[9] which is not without effect among the predominantly black peoples of Africa. And State propaganda for Africa has on occasion included attacks against the missionary tradition as an arm of Western imperialism and exploitation.[10]

Church attempts to gain influence in South America have been exceedingly cautious, reflecting the general trend of Soviet foreign policy towards Latin America. The African experience apparently served to convince the USSR of the dangers of an overly adventurous foreign policy, for miscalculations and the general political instability of the new countries occasioned many reversals for Soviet interests there. In South America, Soviet policy has been marked by a degree of reserve, with the State apparently willing to exercise restraint until its competent but relatively inexperienced representatives within the Latin American situation can advise lines of action which promise success on pragmatic, rather than theoretical, grounds.

One of the chief problems in implementing such a policy has proved to be Cuba. Considerable efforts have been required, first to maintain some sort of influence on Castro's vehemently individualistic and nationalistic form of Communism, second in overcoming the natural attraction of Chinese influences, and finally in restraining the enthusiasm of Cuban zealots from instigating adventures which might conflict with Soviet designs elsewhere in Latin America. The influence of the Church is all but negligible in the Cuban problem, although churchmen from the USSR have visited Cuba, as have their counterparts from Hungary, and, especially, Czechoslovakia.[11]

Argentina offers one of the few natural opportunities for Russian

Orthodox influence, due to the large number of Russian émigrés who have settled there. The Moscow Patriarchate retains a small number of parishes in Argentina, and, on one occasion at least, this outpost was visited by the Patriarchate's Exarch in New York, Archbishop John (Wendland).[12] However, because of the strong residuum of Argentine sympathy for the Nazis in World War II, the Russian emigration may be expected to incline towards anti-Communism (it will be recalled that the Karlovtsy orientation of émigré Orthodoxy supported Hitler), and the Patriarchate's opportunities for effective influence are small. As a result, the Argentine outpost has devoted much effort to influencing non-Orthodox Christians, particularly Roman Catholics.[13]

Elsewhere in Latin America, however, the Churches of the USSR would appear to enjoy no opportunities for effective interchange whatsoever. Countries which do not maintain diplomatic relations with the USSR remain outside the purview of the Moscow Patriarchate; and those countries which do recognize the USSR (Brazil, Chile, Colombia, Mexico, Peru, Uruguay) also seem to be effectively closed to the Russian Churches. In Chile, for example, even though Salvador Allende and his Frente de Accion Popular had represented a major force in the country's political life at least since the elections of 1964, the Russian Church had established virtually no viable contacts with Chilean Christians prior to Allende's election victory in 1970.

The Churches have lent a measure of support to general Soviet propaganda concerning South America. Radical Catholic priests have received some notice in Church journals, and the US intervention in the Dominican Republic was heartily denounced.[14] The general tenor of attacks against Roman Catholicism, when this theme was fashionable in the Russian Church, was to a degree applicable to the Latin American situation.

The chief factor inhibiting any energetic employment of religious influence in South America is the overwhelming predominance of Catholicism. The policy of Soviet hostility to Rome precluded any significant activity by the Russian Church in South America, and, indeed, recent sentiments towards *rapprochement* with Rome may be motivated, in large measure, by the need to provide the Soviet State and the Russian Church with some access to South America.

As the sixties drew to a close, progressive and radical voices within the Catholic majorities in South American countries became an increasingly significant factor. The USSR began to devote considerable attention to this phenomenon and the potential opportunities which could be discerned in it.

Left Catholicism is developing rapidly in our days. The facts of political life in 1967–1969 (the activization of the work of the left movements in the Christian-Democratic parties of Chile, Venezuela, and the exceedingly sharp disagreement between the Church and the dictatorial regime in Brazil; mass demonstrations in workers' quarters of Buenos Aires in support of the daring hierarch, the left Bishop Podest, and the withdrawal of the Christian Democrats from the Government in Peru; the activization of preparedness for a continent-wide meeting of Catholic revolutionaries in Montevideo, the energetic performances of young Catholics—representatives of youth organizations of Colombia, Chile, Peru, Equador, Uruguay, Mexico, and Argentina—for the creation of structural transformation in Latin America, in particular for the rapid establishment of integral agrarian reforms on a broad scale; the decision of the Catholic Church of Brazil to distribute all its lands which have private farmers, poor peasants, and others on them) speak fairly convincingly of the development of the progressiveness of these tendencies.[15]

The potentials for enlisting such sympathies in the work of the Communist movements on the continent were duly noted. The radical Catholic priest, Camilo Torres, for example, was approvingly quoted : ' Communists are revolutionaries. It is precisely with them that movements of unity must be established in order to accomplish the revolution. I shall never become an anti-Communist.' [16] Less extreme advocates of reform within Latin American Catholicism have also received favourable publicity.[17]

In Asia the competition for influence has been especially keen : for not only does the West enjoy the advantages, already mentioned, of the colonial tradition; ethnically and ideologically the area is a natural sphere of influence for China. As will become apparent in the following chapter, the major struggle for influence in the area is in the sphere of Buddhism, and, to a lesser extent, Islam. For the Christian Churches of the USSR there are many problems, since the Christian minorities in the Far East, while enjoying an influence in their countries which is often out of proportion to their numerical strength (due to the educational advantages many of them have enjoyed), are with very few exceptions the offspring of the centuries of Western Christian missionary effort. Prior to the Revolution, the Russian Orthodox Church played a small role in establishing missionary enterprises in the Far East, and the overwhelming majority of the Christian communities in the area are oriented towards Western Christianity. This fact, combined with the dominance of China and the West throughout the area in the post-war period, presents Russian Christianity with a very serious challenge indeed in seeking to build for itself a role in Far Eastern religious affairs.

The Russian Orthodox Church has devoted some attention to Asian affairs, although its opportunities for influence are circumscribed. Because of the British influence, India can be reached through the Christian Churches to some small degree, and, in particular, the Orthodox minority on the subcontinent offers some opportunity to the Russian Church. The Malabar Church, which claims 1,000 churches with 1,500,000 members, has participated in a number of exchanges with the Moscow Patriarchate.[18] The fact that this ancient, non-Chalcedonian Orthodox Church has most of its strength in the State of Kerala, which is also the locus of the strongest Communist sentiments in India, offers a natural basis on which the Russian Church can co-operate with Soviet foreign policy.

The major opportunity for increasing Soviet influence in the Far East, of course, has been the Vietnam conflict. The natural affinities of North Vietnam with China have been eroded considerably by the preponderance of the Soviet economy's ability to provide practical, in addition to moral, support, and such support is duly noted by those large elements in South and Southeast Asia which are apprehensive about continued Western domination. The immense efforts of the CPC with regard to Vietnam have already been mentioned. In addition, the individual Churches have also made enormous contributions to the protest against American involvement. Telegrams to heads of State, protests to international organizations, and appeals to Christian bodies have been ubiquitous in the Moscow Patriarchate's conduct of foreign relations throughout the war. In addition, the Church has been able to make some small contribution to welcoming secular visitors from North Vietnam, and material aid has been given to the NLF and to the North Vietnamese.[19]

Religion has also played a very minor role in the Sino-Soviet dispute, despite the fact that the conflict has been expressed in terms of Marxist, rather than Christian, theology. At the Christian Peace Conference's First All Christian Peace Assembly in 1961, the delegate from China, Bishop Ting, was so unrestrained in his anti-Western diatribes as to endanger the movement's skilful and subtle design for attracting non-Communists, and by 1964 the Chinese Churches had been successfully excluded. The secular press of the USSR occasionally attacks Chinese persecution of religion, particularly in Tibet, and has made capital out of the Chinese attempt to suppress Islam, which has resulted in a mass exodus of Moslems from China across the Sinkiang border into the USSR.[20] Conversely, however, the suppression of the few remaining Christian communities in China during the Cultural Revolution has played no significant role in Soviet propaganda against China.

At the close of the decade, other countries of the Far East were beginning to make an appearance in the foreign affairs of the Russian Churches, but only experimentally and on a rather tentative scale. After the Baptist World Alliance meeting in Japan in 1970, for example, the Russian delegation made a tour of the Far East on their journey home, visiting Christian communities in Bangkok and Rangoon. This visit engendered much goodwill, particularly in Burma, for this was the first occasion on which Baptists from the USSR had visited their fellows in the Far East.

The rise of Japan as the dominant economic power in the Far East, increasingly independent in its outlook, was perhaps the most vital factor in the development of the Far East during the sixties, at least from the point of view of evaluating the trend of the future throughout the area. Soviet foreign policy has been increasingly alert to this phenomenon. The role of religion in the extension of Japanese influence has been duly noted; for example, on 7 December 1969 in an article on Japanese relations with South Korea, *Izvestiia* noted:

The leading role at present is played by economic and spiritual subjugation. Religious and other sorts of ideological organizations are marching at the head as a vanguard for the colonizers. The Japanese have founded hundreds of prayer communes, schools, courses, clubs and publishing concerns in South Korea.

Numerous difficulties confront Soviet foreign policy in assessing the role of religion in Japan and in discovering opportunities for its enlistment in support of Soviet desires. In contrast to the general treatment of religion, which seldom attempts to mask the regime's ideological hostility, treatment of Japanese religions in the Soviet press has usually been remarkably restrained, neutral or even positive in its coverage.[21] The dominant religions (Shinto, Zen Buddhism, etc.), while ultimately deriving from the Buddhist tradition, seem so thoroughly adapted to the specific traditions of Japanese culture, and are so deeply imbued with Japanese nationalism, that few opportunities for uniting with them in common action seem available, whether on a secular level or through the good offices of the Buddhist community of the USSR. The so-called New Religions of Japan—Tenrikyo, Sokka Gakai, Rissho Koseikai, and so on—have been scrutinized by Soviet authors,[22] and, in certain respects, it may be that somewhat better prospects exist among them.

The Russian Churches have not neglected opportunities to join in the search for means of exercising a presence in Japan. Russian Orthodox clerics have visited the country a number of times.[23] At the World Conference on Religion and Peace in Kyoto in October 1970, which was co-sponsored by Rissho Koseikai, a large Soviet delegation was present (six Orthodox members and two each from the Baptist, Muslim, and Buddhist organizations) and made an excellent impression by their courteous, conciliatory deportment. Earlier in 1970 the Moscow Patriarchate had initiated a major realignment in its relations with the Japanese Orthodox Church (the offspring of pre-revolutionary Russian Orthodox missions). As a part of the agreement whereby the US Metropolia received autocephaly,[24] any American jurisdictional relations with the Japanese Orthodox Church were terminated, and the latter became an Autonomous Orthodox Church under the jurisdictional sanction of the Moscow Patriarchate.[25] This seemed highly beneficial to the interests of the Japanese Church, for the jurisdictional relationship with Moscow did not involve major structural limitations on its freedom. In the immediate future, the Japanese Church would have to seek the co-operation of the mother Church in the matter of episcopal ordination: there were only two consecrated Bishops in the Japanese Orthodox Church, and inasmuch as tradition stipulates that three Bishops are required for episcopal ordination, the co-operation of Moscow would have to be sought for the ordination of a third Japanese Bishop. With that hurdle overcome, however, the Japanese Church could conceivably aspire to the absolute independence of autocephalous status. But despite the genuine freedom achieved by the Japanese Church, the Moscow Patriarchate could look forward to an increase in its influence there, if only because of the goodwill attendant upon its generosity in granting autonomy, and if the initial warmth could be maintained and increased, a good basis for harmonious relations could be established. In view of the increasing Soviet recognition of Japan's commanding role in Far Eastern affairs, such warm relations between the Russian Church and the Orthodox minority in Japan, small though that community may be, would not be totally irrelevant to the interests of Soviet foreign policy.

The USSR has enjoyed massive success in altering the balance of power in the Middle East. Since the mid-fifties consistent energy and great resources have been devoted to courting Arab sentiments, in the desire to reduce Western influence in the area in every way possible. The results so far achieved have been immense. The Middle East is no longer the exclusive preserve of the Western powers, and if the vital petroleum resources of the area have not yet been denied to the West, current sentiments place continued Western enjoyment of these resources in some doubt. The Mediterranean Sea has been transformed from an American lake into a theatre of operation of a Soviet fleet of increasing size and sophistication. Perhaps most important, traditional US support of Israel has been brought into sharp conflict with American interests in the other countries of the Middle East, creating a dilemma for the USSR's major competitor which seems insoluble.

Religion has played a relatively small role in Soviet achievements in the Middle East. Because Islam enjoys almost universal adherence throughout the area, the long experience of the Christian Churches in assisting Soviet foreign policy is largely inapplicable. Instead, it is the Muslim religious institutions of the USSR which must provide the bulk of the religious adjunct to Soviet Middle Eastern policy, as will become apparent in the following chapter.

There remains some opportunity for effective employment of Russian Orthodox services in the Middle East, particularly on the eastern littoral of the Mediterranean. In Turkey, relations of the Moscow Patriarchate with the Ecumenical Patriarch can have some inverse effect in influencing the political sentiments of the country, as will be shown in a later chapter. In Syria, the Patriarchate of Antioch influences a small minority which at times can be of some interest to the government, while in Lebanon the Orthodox minority is highly influential. Because of its largely European background, Israel is by no means completely insensitive to its relations with Christians abroad, and the existence of the Patriarchate of Jerusalem insures that Orthodoxy will retain a voice, however small, in the affairs of the region. Finally, the Patriarchate of Alexandria and the Coptic minority maintain a Christian presence in the United Arab Republic.

It would appear that Middle Eastern Church activities, which had been allowed almost to lapse during the latter years of Stalin's rule, have resumed their importance in the foreign affairs of the Russian Orthodox Church. Just as the Church's initial baptism into a vigorous involvement in Soviet foreign policy was inaugurated by Patriarch Aleksii's tour of the Middle East in 1945, so the expanded activity of the sixties was preceded by a second tour in 1960.[26] Patriarch Aleksii visited Damascus, Beirut, Jordan and Jerusalem, Cairo and Alexandria on this visit, and he concluded it—unlike his tour of 1945—by a lengthy conference with the Ecumenical Patriarch in Istanbul and a visit to Athens before returning to Moscow. The subsequent decade would demonstrate that the tour was motivated primarily by pan-Orthodox considerations, but it also served to inaugurate a degree of participation in Middle Eastern affairs which was not irrelevant to Soviet foreign policy interests in the area.

The twin foci of Russian Orthodox participation in Soviet efforts to extend influence in the Middle East were the Patriarchates of Antioch and Jerusalem. Numerous visits were made to the former, and in 1966 the Moscow Patriarchate participated in the dedication of a Church in Damascus and a hospital and its equipment in Beirut, both gifts of the Russian Orthodox Church to the Patriarchate of Antioch.[27] Jerusalem was the recipient of even more attention. The Russian Orthodox Mission in Jerusalem received much support and, indeed, rendered valuable service by providing some of the future leaders of Russian Orthodox international activities, chief among them Nikodim, with their initial experience in the conduct of foreign affairs. In 1964 the first Russian Orthodox Easter pilgrimage to the Holy Land in fifty-five years took place,[28] and thereafter a pilgrimage became an annual event, allowing numerous of the junior affiliates of the Moscow Patriarchate's Department of External Church Relations to gain some experience in international affairs, and serving as a means for maintaining close relations with the Patriarchate of Jerusalem. Infrequently the Moscow Patriarchate would raise the issue of Russian properties in Jerusalem, some of which, especially in the Jordanian sector, remained in the possession of the hostile Synod Abroad of the émigré Russian Church. In addition, in 1966 a Russian delegation visited a monastery in Sinai, a part of the UAR at the time.[29]

However valuable such services may have been, they remained all but negligible in comparison with the vast efforts Soviet foreign policy was devoting to the area, as became apparent during the Six-Day War between Israel and the Arab States early in June 1967. Incongruously, the Church, traditionally instant in support of Soviet interests in such crises, remained silent during and immediately after the war. This silence prevailed, almost without exception, throughout the Churches of Eastern Europe and the USSR, despite the fact that the secular press in these areas engaged in a massive attack against Israeli and US aggression. Curiously enough, it was the Jews in the German Democratic Republic who provided one of the few exceptions to the silence which prevailed in religious circles; prominent Jews signed a statement on 10 June condemning Israel:

After all the terrible experiences of the past the rulers of Israel are not satisfied at having entered a disastrous and unnatural alliance with imperialism. Moreover, they are closely and quite openly collaborating with the Nazi murderers of the Jewish people, in other words with the West German imperialists in Bonn. For many years the West German imperialists have been helping to build up the potential of Israeli aggression by shipments of arms, training of military cadres by Nazi generals and the creation of a war industry in Israel . . .

.   .   .   .

It is the policy of aggression which endangers the existence of the State of Israel and the lives of all its citizens. He who lives on an island should not make an enemy of the Ocean. There will be peace in the Near East only when the Government of Israel gives up its imperialist policy and finally returns to one of good will and neighbourliness toward, and respect for, the interests of the Arab nations.[30]

There are several factors which help to explain the State's failure to attempt to utilize the Churches in its campaign of support of the defeated Arabs. Most important is the obvious fact that such support could have little effect in strengthening Soviet influence among the Arabs, and might even risk a contra-productive effect. The Arabs, with some justification, were equating Christianity with pro-Israeli sentiment, and to elicit support from a part of the Christian Church might serve to dilute the rampant hostility of the Arabs towards the real or imagined Judaeo-Christian *entente* threatening their interests. Secondly, the issue offered very little promise for success in the Western Churches; unlike peace, which could draw upon the strong stream of pacifism throughout Christendom, the Six-Day War offered no pre-existing basis on which anti-Israeli sentiments could be elicited. Finally, to attract increased attention in the Churches to the Soviet involvement in the dispute might have resulted in alerting the Churches to the plight of the Jews in Eastern Europe and the USSR, for the events in the Middle East were followed by a period of vigorous attack against Jews domestically, motivated, in part, by a possible desire to demonstrate to the Arab States that the USSR and its allies were without reservation in support of their cause.

Belatedly, the Churches were brought into the dispute in a tangential way. On 4 July the Working Committee of the CPC, meeting in Zagorsk, near Moscow, issued a statement supporting the Soviet position on the events in the Middle East, and in November Hromadka and others indulged in self-criticism for the CPC's failure to devote more attention to the problem. On 22 February 1968 Nikodim generated a small amount of publicity against Israel by sending a telegram to the President of Israel protesting against incidents endangering Russian Orthodox properties, and to the answering telegram denying that such incidents had taken place he replied with a letter, with copies to World Council of Churches leaders, on 7 April giving specifics (referring to six incidents in 1964 and 1966, and none subsequently).[31]

In summary, the endeavours of the Church have been of service to Soviet foreign policy in the Third World in a wide variety of ways. The chief area of service has been in the Vietnam confrontation, which has, together with the Cuban revolution and the continuing penetration of the Middle East, provided Soviet interests with their most spectacular successes of the post-Stalin era. In addition to the Vietnam issue, however, religion has augmented Soviet activities in many different ways, always peripheral but nonetheless beneficial, and the Churches have a broad range of opportunities for rendering further service to Soviet foreign policy in the Third World.

6 Islam and Buddhism

THE Muslim world has loomed large in the Soviet evaluaton of its foreign opportunities and obligations almost from the inception of the Soviet State. In one of its early policy statements in 1917, the fledgling Soviet regime addressed a proclamation to 'Muslims of the East, Persians and Turks, Arabs and Hindus', categorically renouncing any and all claims which had been tendered by the former government of the Russian Empire.[1] Formally, at least, Islam became the first of the world's great religions which figured specifically in the planning and discussion of Soviet foreign policy. In 1918, a 'Union for the Liberation of the East' was established,[2] and in September 1920, a week-long conference of representatives from Eastern countries was held in Baku, to which a number of Muslim dignitaries were invited.[3] In 1923 and 1924, conferences of Muslim clergy were held in Baku and Tashkent, which issued appeals to other Muslims against the British and in favour of the Soviet Union.[4]

During all these years an animated debate raged in Communist circles concerning the Muslim world. Much of the substance of the controversies was somewhat arcane, concerning the basic position the Muslim world should occupy in the light of Marxist doctrine; as the imminence of revolution in Germany and the advanced nations receded, to some of the Marxist adepts it appeared that the Muslim world might be next on the agenda of history's inevitable progression towards Communism. The bulk of the argumentation was not especially relevant to the specific question of the international role of the Muslim religion—indeed, history has treated somewhat unkindly most, if not all, of the confident prognostications of these early attempts at a Marxist divination of the future. Nevertheless, the debate did at times attempt to grapple with Islam as a religion, and there were elements who proposed that because of its unique features, Islam can be considered progressive and, indeed, presents an opportunity which must be seized upon in the attempt to extend the influence of Communism abroad.

The debate was especially vigorous in the Comintern. At the Second and Third Congresses (1923 and 1925), there was heated discussion of the proper attitude towards Pan-Islamic tendencies, even though the Soviet government was inclined to view such movements askance. Tan

Makala, the Communist leader from Indonesia, argued that the all-embracing character of Islam, involving every aspect of the life of Muslim peoples, was not merely religious, but represented a veritable struggle for liberation throughout the colonial world, and as such it merited the fullest support and collaboration of all Communists. He pointed in particular to Indonesia and India as areas illustrative of his thesis.[5] The Soviet leaders, however, found it inexpedient to acquiesce wholeheartedly, for a number of reasons. One fundamental disability under which they had to operate was ignorance; it would be several decades before the Soviet Union could lay claim to any kind of competence in scholarship on the world outside, and as a result the leaders had to work their way through a maze of conflicting reports, many of them from non-Communist (and hence suspect) sources. Perhaps more crippling was a natural myopia which affected the Soviet leaders, almost to a man. The Muslim populations of Soviet Central Asia were an immense problem at the time, and thus domestic considerations provided most of the colouration of Moscow's picture of Islam. In particular, any pan-Islamic sympathies could only promise trouble for the Soviet regime; as with the Pan-Turkish movement, such supranationalistic aspirations could not but complicate the problem of the Soviet Union in securing the affections of its Muslim peoples, many of them of Turkic extraction.

Indeed, in many respects the content of the word ' Muslim ' was, for the Soviet leaders, largely confined to Turkey and Persia. The USSR expressed warm approval of the Jangali revolt in Persia, despite its strong religious overtones,[6] and for many years great hopes were placed on the events taking place in Turkey and, to a lesser extent, Afghanistan. The Arab world, however, seemed nearly invisible to the eyes of the Soviet leadership, and the Muslims at great removes (India, the Pacific basin, etc.) all but non-existent.

With the waning of the 1920s, Soviet policy turned inwards, and for the next decade Islam played no important role in Soviet foreign policy. The Soviet regime engaged in a massive effort to eradicate the influence of Islam (and all other religions) in the country, and this programme was pursued with a single-mindedness which precluded any considerable attempt to utilize religion in foreign affairs. Indeed, with the gathering clouds of war in Europe, the Soviet State had little enough energy to spare for machinations in the Muslim world, especially operations so peripheral to the major interests of diplomacy and economic or military considerations as to involve experimentation with the religions of the non-European world.

The situation was reversed with the advent of World War II. In need of support wherever it might be found, the Soviet government welcomed the services of its religious leaders, and Muslim clergy began to participate in radio broadcasts for foreign consumption and in the preparation of foreign propaganda in support of the Soviet war effort.[7] In particular, Shiite Muslims were encouraged to issue appeals to their Shiite co-religionists in Persia and Iraq. After the war, Muslim clergy were able to benefit from the new policy of limited accommodation from the regime in return for political support, and like their Russian Orthodox counterparts, entered into a programme of fairly vigorous activity in support of Soviet activities in international affairs. Soviet Muslims participated in numerous visits to Muslim countries, to propagate Soviet views in these parts of the world. Pan-Islamism came under attack as a machination of US imperialism.[8] When the peace campaign was initiated, Muslim clerics were to be found at many of its meetings, making their contribution to the proceedings in the accepted idiom of the day. In 1952 the most prominent Muslim cleric in Soviet foreign policy, Zia al-Din Babakhanov, broadcast to the Middle East:

As a Muslim I call on you to support the resolutions [of the World Peace Congress] on the need for the unification of Germany, to support the cause of peace, backing the Japanese people in their struggle against the San Francisco Treaty imposed on them by the USA. I fully endorse the resolutions of the Peking Peace Conference on Korea where the American aggressors under the banner of the UN are exterminating towns, villages and peoples by the use of gas and germ bombs... If the peoples do not take up the cause of peace today, what is happening in Korea will happen in these countries also. I call upon the peoples of the East to prepare for the Vienna Peace Congress.[9]

Despite the frequency with which Muslim clerics made appearances in Soviet foreign affairs, it was not until the death of Stalin that Islam became a truly important adjunct to Soviet foreign policy. The 'two camp' model of the world, whereby nations were divided exactly and without remainder into the Socialist and Capitalist camps, left little room for manoeuvre with regard to the Muslim world; when the post-Stalin regime revised this schema by postulating a third, neutral classification, immense possibilities were instantly available for a religious dimension in Soviet relations with Muslim countries, and Soviet Islam began exploring these opportunities with vigour.

The contribution which Muslims can make to the execution of Soviet foreign policy, while important, is peripheral. The chief service which they can render is in broadening the range of contacts open to the Soviet Union in Muslim countries. While the USSR enjoys ample means of eliciting interest in the underdeveloped countries due to its vaunted economic and military stature, the fact that Muslim people can discover a dimension of shared religious traditions and attitudes is of definite usefulness in cementing relationships. In 1967 one Soviet commentator noted:

In recent years our relations with Arab countries have intensified considerably. I have had occasion to hear from those who have been there that they have easily found a common language with the inhabitants of these countries. ' No sooner did they learn that we are Muslims than our relationships became very warm.' [10]

While he went on to warn that ' it is not fitting for representatives of the countries of Socialism to seek bases for friendship between people in religious adherence ', it is not difficult to imagine that policy-makers in the USSR are not absolutely opposed to utilization of such advantages where they may be found.

A second major service rendered by Muslim participants in foreign affairs is in shielding the USSR from possible untoward reactions to policies applied to Muslims domestically. Even at the best of times during the post-war period, Islam has received only the most limited permission to function in the USSR. The lack of facilities for worship has always been critical; official Soviet sources have claimed 8,000 ' Muslim communities ',[11] although on other occasions they have stated that there were 1,200 mosques,[12] and either figure compares unfavourably with the population of 25–30 million Muslim inhabitants. From the later 1950s onwards Islam has borne its share of the various disabilities attendant upon the general antireligious campaign, and there have been severe reductions in the limited freedom hitherto enjoyed. The number of legally functioning mosques has declined precipitately (to perhaps a total of 400), and nearly every aspect of Muslim life has come under severe pressure. Muslims who participate in Soviet international affairs have rendered an exceedingly useful service—and have enjoyed almost unbroken success—in preventing any accurate assessment of religious conditions within the USSR from developing in the Muslim world.

There have been occasional reversals. In 1966 the Second Islamic Congress in Mecca excoriated the tendency of the Soviet (and Chinese) governments to attempt to destroy the national identity of their Muslim peoples by discrimination against their religion and traditions.[13] Similarly, Turkey, Persia, and Afghanistan have long expressed concern for the situation of related peoples in the USSR.[14] Countermeasures employed by Soviet Muslims would seem more than adequate, however. A National Conference of Moslem Clergy in Tashkent in 1962, for example, attended to such problems.

Participants in the conference stressed the provocative nature of slander concerning the life of Moslems in the USSR, circulated by imperialist propaganda in order to bring about a division within the international Muslim movement for universal peace and friendship among nations.[15]

As early as 1954, a group of Syrian scientists who had made an extended visit to the USSR during the peak of the most intense attack against religion since before the war (prior to the campaign of the sixties), brought back glowing reports on the ' absolute freedom ' of Soviet Muslims.[16] The overall assessment of the degree to which Soviet Muslims have succeeded in shielding domestic affairs from outside purveyance must be immensely favourable, for expressions of concern in the Muslim world have been exceedingly rare, and the general impression of Soviet treatment of domestic Muslims seems to be favourable almost without exception.

Contemporaneously with the increasing use of Muslims in Soviet foreign policy, intensive efforts to develop Soviet scholarship on the world of Islam began almost immediately after the death of Stalin.[17] Prior to the middle 1950s Soviet studies on Muslim areas were, with few exceptions, heavily laced with polemic, and seemed to pay much more attention to the current ideological assessment than to elucidating the actual situation. The results of such careless scholarship were highly detrimental to Soviet foreign policy; this inadequacy played no small part in accounting for the delay of the USSR in recognizing the extent to which opinion had shifted during World War II in the Arab world, for example, and hence Soviet foreign policy was several years late in awakening to the advantages which might be gained there. After the death of Stalin, however, objective, dispassionate scholarship developed rapidly, with the result that for the past decade the USSR has been able to avail itself of accurate information in assessing opportunities in the Muslim world.

Such opportunities are considerable, despite the apparent contradiction between Communism and Islam. Islam is a holistic religion which, unlike Christianity (or at least post-medieval Christianity), permeates every aspect of life. The distinction between the sacred and the profane is largely meaningless, for in practice no aspect of life is considered secular, or even more secular than any other. Politics, economics, and the traditions and mores of all of life are no less permeated with Islam than are worship activities. As a result, a common religious tradition can be effective far beyond the ranks of the professional clergy; a Communist from Soviet Central Asia, devout atheist though he may be, can nevertheless enjoy a considerable advantage in the Muslim world because of the common Muslim tradition. Conversely, Islam provides an effective *entrée* to the highest instances of government in the Muslim world; Muslims are much less impeded by that inability to gain the attention of political leaders which Christians often experience, for a truly secular government is somewhat of a rarity in the Muslim world.

Furthermore, the Soviet Union, which bases its approach on the material advantages which the Soviet system is able to offer (economic and military aid, a model for rapid industrialization, etc.), is able to profit from the temporal emphasis of the Muslim religion. Without denigrating the other virtues and the various rewards awaiting the believer on a post-temporal plane, Islam places immense stress on the virtue of righteousness, interpreted, usually, in a concrete, immediate, social sense. It is obvious that eradication of economic imbalance and poverty is prerequisite to the achievement of temporal righteousness, and Islam balances the private virtue of submission to the provisions of providence with a public commitment to active, energetic achievement of righteousness (including, in extreme instances, the *jihad*, or holy war, for its attainment). In addition, Islam has historically contained a large element of political ambition, equating righteousness with the righteous society and State. The result is that if any foreign power can offer a promise of aid in the achievement of such temporal benefits as are needed, Islam provides considerable incentive for pursuing such advantages, both individually and, more importantly, on a political level.

Perhaps the most significant advantage enjoyed by the USSR in its relations with the Muslim world is to be found in the rampant nationalism which pervades the developing world. Almost without exception, Muslim countries are nationally, rather than ideologically, oriented, and Islam, for all its supranational implications, is interpreted in nationalistic colours. The result is that most of the Muslim states can maintain relationships with the USSR without religious or ideological embarrassment, however much the antireligious ideology of the latter may conflict with their own assessment of the Islamic religion. International relations for Muslim countries are nationalistically conceived, almost exclusively pragmatic in orientation, and if relations with even an atheist country can provide concrete advantages which facilitate the achievement of that righteous society demanded by Islam, they can be entered into with impunity. This is especially so if overtones, however peripheral, of a community of religious traditions can be found with a portion of that country's population.

Muslim participation in Soviet foreign policy has been increasingly vigorous throughout the post-Stalin period. A kaleidoscopic array of activities has been initiated on numerous levels, clerical and lay. Even to enumerate the concrete relationships which have developed between Soviet and foreign Muslims would be a formidable task, and in the interests of economy, this study must remain content with an illustrative, rather than an exhaustive, survey.

After the rupture with the People's Republic of China, when the Sino-Soviet dispute became public and unrestrained, the Soviet regime occasionally utilized Chinese maltreatment of Muslims in its propaganda arsenal. Both injustices to predominantly Muslim national minorities [18] and, more rarely, Chinese discrimination against the Islamic religion as such were attacked.[19] In support of their accusations the Soviet commentators could point to concrete evidence of the intensity of the Chinese campaign against the Muslim minorities, for as early as in 1966 a half million Muslims had fled across the Sinkiang border to Soviet Central Asia,[20] where conditions were immensely more tolerable despite the vigorous campaign against Islam which the Soviet regime was itself waging at the time, and this flow of Muslims into the USSR from China has continued in increasing numbers.

In the Western Pacific basin, Soviet exploitation of Islam has been somewhat muted, for only recently has the USSR begun to acquire the logistical capabilities necessary to a vigorous foreign policy in this comparatively remote part of the world. On occasion, Soviet foreign propaganda has turned its attention to Muslims in the Philippines, berating the Ismailites for alleged subordination to British imperialism through the Aga Khan.[21] Relations with Indonesia were somewhat stronger. As early as in 1956, President Sukarno was granted an audience with the Chief Mufti of Central Asia and Kazakhstan during his visit to Tashkent,[22] and Soviet participation at Muslim gatherings in Indonesia was vigorous. However, it should be noted that with the development of the Sino-Soviet schism, the USSR found itself in a secondary position in Indonesia, for China, with its enormous Muslim population, relative physical proximity, and glamorous commitment to revolutionary militance, was immensely better equipped to use the Muslim element in Indonesia. After the *putsch* in 1965 relations between Soviet and Indonesian Muslims weakened in conformity with the general collapse of Soviet relations with the country, and there were no signs of attempts to rebuild these Muslim relations. At least from a formal point of view, ample opportunities remained, and, indeed, Islam would seem to represent one of the very few avenues of approach still open—other possibilities seem to be minimal in Indonesia, which after 1965 began leaning rather strongly towards the West. Chief among the five basic principles which the Suharto government took as its guidelines is the assertion of the unity of God, by which relations with avowedly atheistic countries are specifically eschewed. Should Muslims from the USSR contrive to do in Indonesia what they have in the past done with some success elsewhere, i.e. to demonstrate that the atheism of the Soviet government is more formal than actual, as witness the felicitous conditions which Soviet Muslims are said to enjoy, then possibly at least some of the popular—and, perhaps, even official—prejudice against the USSR might be eroded. At the end of the sixties, however, this line of approach remained a mere potential, for the Soviet regime maintained a highly sceptical attitude towards Indonesia after 1965.

On the Southeast Asian mainland, with the possible exception of Malaysia, Islam is not very strong, and Soviet utilization of religion was confined to other faiths. Similarly, in the South Asian subcontinent, India presented relatively little opportunity, for the predominant Hindu religion has little or no parallel in the Soviet population. Even after the post-war partitioning of the country, however, India retained a Muslim minority more numerous than that in the USSR, and on occasion Indian Muslims were invited to visit their counterparts in Central Asia.[23] Pakistan, which is officially Islamic and whose population is almost exclusively Muslim, would offer greater opportunities to Soviet Islam. However, until late in the 1960s the country was all but closed to the USSR, first because of its membership of the Baghdad Pact, and then because of its alignment with China until well after the Kashmir War in 1965. Only at the end of the sixties did the Soviet Union enjoy some success at establishing a twofold relationship on the subcontinent, with equally good relations with both India and Pakistan, despite their internecine rivalry. As a result of this initiation of more congenial relationships, the Muslim dimension of Soviet foreign policy towards Pakistan began to be intensified, with such customary exercises as the entertainment of delegations of Pakistani Muslims in the USSR.[24]

Relations with Turkish, Persian, and Afghan Muslims have enjoyed no spectacular successes. The hopes of an earlier generation have proved to be fruitless, for both Turkey and Iran have generally sought alignment with the West due to such factors as the success of the Marshall Plan in Turkey and the tactical errors of Soviet attempts at penetration of Iranian territories. The nascent signs of *rapprochement* with Turkey might offer some promise of future gains, but it should be remembered that Turkey, despite its recognition of Islam as the dominant religion, attempts to the degree possible to divorce religion from the official decisions of the government.

It is in the Arab world that Soviet foreign policy has secured the greatest achievements of the post-war period, and Islam has played a vigorous supporting role in the successful execution of Soviet policy towards the Arab States. Even antireligious journalism in the USSR has admitted the usefulness of Islam to Soviet endeavours in the Arab world.[25] There have remained pockets of resistance to Soviet Middle Eastern influences, primarily in those few States which have resisted Soviet blandishments and have maintained their alignment with the West, such as Saudi Arabia. The unfavourable views of Soviet treatment of Muslims at the Mecca conference in 1966 have already been mentioned. A greater problem was presented by the attempts of Saudi Arabia to form a Pan-Islamic Alliance in the middle sixties. The USSR interpreted these attempts as a thinly veiled attempt by American and British imperialism to buttress their hegemony in the Arab world,[26] and their analyses were outspokenly hostile.

The Islamic Alliance scheme takes into account the fact that most of the people in the UAR, Syria, Algeria and other Arab countries are Moslems. Its sponsors mean to take advantage of this to raise another 'wall' against progressive ideas in the Middle East. They are out to counter these ideas with laws of the Koran, and hope that in the event of success the profound socio-economic transformations and reforms undertaken in the UAR, Algeria and Syria will fade away. They pin particular hopes on the difficulties arising in these countries in the process of their economic and social reconstruction.[27]

As things turned out, the projected Islamic Alliance never bore fruit, but it should be noted that the major cause for the plan's frustration was not Soviet hostility, but rather the insuperable problems of nationalism within the Arab world.

Egypt has been the chief focus of Soviet foreign policy in the Middle East since the mid-1950s, and, indeed, the bulk of the spectacular success won by the USSR in the Arab world has accrued in its relations with Egypt. Soviet Muslims have played an active role in support of these relations, devoting great effort and much energy to establishing and cementing warm relations with their fellow-believers from the UAR. As early as in 1955–6, a small group of Muslim theological students from the USSR was allowed to enrol at the prestigious Azhar University in Cairo, thereby becoming the first Soviet citizens in history to be allowed to pursue theological studies outside the Soviet Union.[28] President Nasser himself was entertained by the Chief Mufti during his visit to Tashkent in 1958.[29] Soviet Muslims contributed vigorously to the propaganda campaign in support of Egypt occasioned by the Suez crisis in 1956,[30] and again in connection with the Six-Day War of 1967 the voice of Soviet Islam was prominent in support of the Arab cause. The annual pilgrimages from the USSR to Mecca have habitually included extended visits to the UAR, and visits by Muslim dignitaries from the UAR to the USSR have been frequent. In 1970, for example, a delegation of Muslim religious leaders from the UAR, led by the Grand Sheikh Mohammed el-Fakham, Rector of al-Azhar University, made an extended visit to the USSR at the invitation of the Ecclesiastical Administration of the Muslims of Central Asia and Kazakhstan.[31]

In Syria efforts to utilize Muslim sentiments have been no less vigorous. Even though the Baath regimes in Syria and Iraq are secularist, they continue to recognize Islam as the State religion and Islamic religious traditions as the source of law,[32] and hence there remains ample opportunity for the exercise of a religious dimension in Soviet policy towards such countries. Some difficulties may be expected due to the fact that Syrian Muslims adhere to the Shiite branch of Islam, rather than to the Sunnite branch, as in Egypt,[33] and because Shiite Muslims are less numerous in the USSR and somewhat less well organized, the domestic base for the utilization of Islam in Soviet foreign policy is comparatively weak. Nevertheless, the USSR has not ignored the Muslim component in the popular sentiments of Syria, which, together with Egypt, has been the locus of the most pronounced interest in the Soviet experiment in Socialism since World War II. Not only has the normal flow of contacts and visitors between the USSR and

Syria been employed, the USSR has on occasion devised some rather novel experiments in eliciting desirable responses from Syria. In 1957, for example, Soviet Muslim leaders protested strongly against an incident of 'Turkish armed aggression in Syria', which subsequently proved to be wholly imaginary.[34] The Syrian Sheikh Muhammed al-Ashmar was awarded an International Lenin Prize in 1958 'for strengthening peace between peoples', while similar personages from Iraq and the Sudan have also been singled out for praise.[35] Syrian reversals in the 1967 war received due notice in the propaganda of Soviet Muslims surrounding that event.

The activities of Soviet Muslims have been somewhat less visible elsewhere in the Arab world, although nearly every non-aligned Arab country (Iraq, the Sudan, Somalia, Algeria—which was accused of maltreatment of Muslims in 1958 [36]—Jordan) has been the recipient of visits and exchanges, has received support in Soviet propaganda oriented towards Muslims, and the like. Muslims have also contributed to Soviet propaganda concerning problems with little or no direct Muslim significance. For example, at a meeting of the Soviet Afro-Asian Solidarity Committee in 1960, Babakhanov declared:

> The Muslims in the USSR pour scorn on the actions of the imperialist aggressors in the Congo Republic. The peoples of Asia and Africa must see to it that the imperialists, headed by the American neo-colonisers, leave the Congo immediately and give its people a real opportunity to settle their fate themselves.[37]

The range of Soviet activities in the Muslim field extends far beyond the personal diplomacy of visits and the realm of normal propaganda. In the 1950s Soviet Muslims sent monetary gifts to the needy in the wake of the Suez crisis and of floods in Pakistan.[38] In 1959 an edition of the Koran was published in Tashkent which, despite its limited number (fewer than 5,000 copies), was made available to foreign Muslims on numerous occasions.[39] Soviet leaders have been careful to send Muslim New Year's greetings to the Islamic world.[40] In 1966, for example, Brezhnev, Kosygin, and Podgorny sent a telegram of greetings to Nasser, while Kosygin and Podgorny sent New Year greetings telegrams to Algeria, the UAR, the Yemen, Iraq, Syria, Mauritania, Tunisia, Jordan, Libya, the Lebanon, Morocco, the Sudan, Somalia, Kuwait, and Saudi Arabia.[41]

Of special significance, both for propaganda value and in providing the occasion for numerous visits in the Arab world, is the annual *hadj*, or pilgrimage to Mecca. The first group to make the *hadj* did so in 1944, with aircraft provided by the Soviet government.[42] Only very small numbers were given permission to participate, and the *hadj* remained a most uncertain event in Stalin's years. In 1946, for example, 17 of 200 applicants were granted permission, but apparently the trip was cancelled due to failure to obtain visas; in 1947, the planned pilgrimage of 40 approved applicants was finally cancelled, the reason given as failure to obtain transit visas from Turkey and Iran, or, alternatively, a cholera epidemic.[43] Immediately upon the death of Stalin, the *hadj* was renewed in 1953,[44] and thereafter it became an annual event, in which a small group of selected Muslim citizens of the USSR were despatched to the Arab world and succeeded in amassing a considerable store of goodwill and favourable publicity from their trips.

Soviet Muslims have also devoted great energies to participation in international conferences, where their efforts can hope to achieve a wholesale effect of some impact throughout the Muslim world and beyond. Muslims from the USSR have frequently served at general conferences such as those on Disarmament, the World Congress of Religions in Delhi in 1958,[45] or the World Conference on Religion and Peace in Kyoto in 1970. The Tashkent conference in 1962 sent a letter of thanks to Khrushchev 'for the courage and restraint that he displayed over the Cuban crisis'.[46] Soviet Muslims were among the 120 delegates at the Sixth World Islamic Congress in Mogadishu, Somalia, in 1964 and, indeed, experienced a moment of slight embarrassment: 'A provocatory question concerning the position of Muslims in the USSR, originally introduced for discussion, under the pressure of the majority of the delegates was excluded from the agenda.' [47] Nor was all felicitous for the Soviet participants thereafter: 'Many delegates expressed serious disturbance in connection with the ever widening dissemination of the idea of scientific Socialism among the Muslim population.' [48] At the First Afro-Asian Islamic Conference in Bandung, Indonesia, in 1965, the Soviet delegation made an excellent impression on the Arab delegates, due, in part, to their fluent command of Arabic. The status of the Soviet delegation was in some doubt at first:

In the course of the conference certain delegates again raised the question of the competence of the delegation of Soviet Muslims to participate, in connection with the allegation that the Soviet Union is neither an African nor an Asian country. However, the overwhelming majority of the votes (30 to 4) supported the Soviet Union's belonging to the Asian countries.[49]

Having weathered this challenge, the Soviet delegation then asked for full-member status, in place of their assigned role as observers. A further illustration of this style of activity took place in October 1970:

A three-day conference of representatives of Muslims residing in the USSR took place in Tashkent. Religious leaders from 24 countries—including the UAR, the Syrian Arab Republic, the Iraqi Republic, the Yemen Arab Republic, the People's Republic of Southern Yemen, Sudan, Somalia, Lebanon, Afghanistan, Iran, Morocco, Ceylon, Guyana and the Philippines—attended. The conference motto was 'For Unity and Co-operation in the Struggle for Peace.' . . .

The conference participants adopted three documents containing constructive proposals for the worldwide defense and strengthening of peace.

A message addressed to all Muslims and men of good will paid particular attention to the events in the Near East. The message stated that imperialist powers—primarily the USA and its political tool, the ruling circles of Israel—bear full responsibility for the dangerous situation in that area.[50]

In summary, Islam has played a vigorous and effective role in Soviet foreign policy throughout the post-war period. Particularly since the death of Stalin, Soviet Muslims have engaged in a wide variety of activities, covering the extent of the geographic limits of the Muslim world. To some degree, the enormous success which the USSR has enjoyed in establishing its influence in the Muslim—and particularly the Arab—world has been facilitated by the effective services which have been rendered by the Muslims of the Soviet Union.

One final note may be in order concerning a recent American candidate for membership of the world of Islam. The Black Muslims of the US have been noted on occasion in the Soviet press, but it would not seem that this new religion is viewed as a religion at all by the USSR, but instead as a rather aberrational—and perhaps somewhat quaint—political expression of the social tensions in the US.[51] Certainly no overt attempts by Soviet Muslim leaders to explore any sort of religious relationships with the American Black Muslims have been initiated.

Buddhism, in contrast to Islam, has not played nearly so extensive a role in Soviet foreign policy. Whereas the Muslim community has emulated the Russian Orthodox Church in maintaining a small corps of specialists employed almost constantly in international affairs, Buddhism's role has been more sporadic, with Buddhists appearing in the international arena more infrequently.

There are a number of reasons for this apparent neglect of Buddhism in Soviet foreign policy. One of the fundamental difficulties encountered in any attempt to mobilize the Buddhist religion for political ends is that Buddhism offers relatively few obvious opportunities for political utilization. Buddhism is intensely individual in its emphasis, concentrating primarily on the means of overcoming the vicissitudes of life on an individual basis. The religion's organizational structure is somewhat amorphous: Theravada (Hinayana) Buddhism, which is the more philosophical branch, concentrates almost exclusively on the development of individual virtue, and such professional services as it may employ from clerical ranks are minimal, while even the more highly organized forms of Mahayana Buddhism operate with a structure far removed from the hierarchical formations common to Christianity. Hence Buddhism's impact on political life is likely to take forms of individual, rather than corporate or institutional, persuasion, rendering the task of initiating an effective alliance with the religion for political ends exceedingly complex.

Furthermore, Buddhism is permeated with a general tone of pessimism regarding temporal existence. Suffering is taken to be inevitable, and it is the task of the Buddhist, applying the disciplines of the faith individually, to achieve release from the chimeras and sufferings of mundane existence. A social component to Buddhist theology is all but absent, and even contemporary attempts to rectify such an omission find their expression primarily in appealing for individual political leaders of Buddhist persuasion to seek amelioration of social inequities through the application of Buddhist tenets of conduct in their concrete political activities. As a result, broad themes of social aspirations which may be utilized in Soviet foreign policy, such as exist in Christianity and Islam, are minimal in Buddhism. Even the intense theme of pacifism, which might seem at first glance to offer an obvious correlation with Soviet peace activities, proves on inspection to represent an ambiguous advantage at best. Buddhist pacifism is interpreted primarily in individualistic terms, and, more importantly, is directed almost exclusively to non-resistance of evil. To date, at least, Soviet spokesmen have not managed to integrate non-resistance to evil very harmoniously into the search for peace they normally advocate.

More concretely, the Soviet regime suffers from limitations due to the denominational demography within Buddhism. The Soviet Buddhist nationalities adhere exclusively to Lamaist Buddhism, a rather complex and somewhat syncretistic form of Mahayana Buddhism shared by other Central Asian peoples (Mongolians, Tibetans, Nepalese, Sikkimese, etc.). There are significant differences between Lama Buddhism and the other forms of Mahayana Buddhism which are found, primarily, in China and Chinese influenced areas. Ceylon, Burma, and the countries of Southeast Asia are predominantly Theravadic, and the differences between Mahayana and Theravada Buddhism are at least as great as the denominational differences which prevail in the Christian world. Hence effective use of Soviet Buddhists in foreign affairs is complicated by intra-Buddhist differences, reducing somewhat its effectiveness.

In general, Buddhism presents a most complex challenge to the Western political mind, for its reactions to various injustices or potentially catastrophic events are imbued with the peculiar overtones of acceptance and patience more common to the Eastern than to the Western ethos. As a result, Soviet foreign policy, which is no less pragmatic and concrete in its orientation than that of any other European power, may be expected to find in Buddhism a relatively uncongenial atmosphere for the achievement of specific foreign policy ends.

More concrete is the historical disability which Soviet use of Buddhism has suffered in its development due to the Sino-Soviet dispute. Until the late fifties or early sixties, China and the USSR acted in concert in relations with Buddhist countries, and China, because it was immensely better equipped for involvement in Buddhist activities, bore the brunt of the planning and execution of activities designed to elicit Buddhist support for the Communist powers. Even as late as 1959, for example, when tensions with China had long since become obvious (if not yet public), Soviet propaganda mobilized Buddhists from the USSR in support of the Chinese role in the Tibetan uprising.[52] When the Sino-Soviet dispute had become irreconcilable and the rupture open and definitive, however, Soviet foreign policy found itself without a well-developed capability for utilization of Buddhism, and for several years the major role went to the Chinese almost by default.

The most crippling limitation which the USSR suffers with regard to Buddhism is the infinitesimal power base which domestic Buddhism supplies. Buddhism was a relatively late arrival among the nomadic Mongolian peoples of the present-day USSR, and enjoys only some 250 years of tradition among them. The result is that Buddhism has shown only moderate ability to survive the attacks which it has suffered institutionally during the past half-century, and indigenous religious practices have shown a remarkable resurgence in the wake of the deterioration of institutional Buddhism.

Soviet power reached the Buddhist population relatively late; the Buryats, for example, did not come under Soviet administration until 1923. For a brief period a reformist branch of Buddhism, which reacted favourably to the advent of Communism, was active, and, indeed, in 1926 the Congress of Soviet Buddhists sent a telegram to the Dalai Lama in Tibet praising the Soviet regime.[53] This, however, was a lonely instance of co-operation between Buddhists and Soviet foreign policy, and a quarter of a century would elapse before attempts to profit from the services of Soviet Buddhists in international affairs would be resumed.

Late in the twenties Buddhism came under fierce attack in the USSR. In the next decade, Buddhism virtually disappeared as an institution in Soviet society. The active monasteries were closed almost without exception, the large corps of monks was nearly liquidated, and the broad range of Buddhist traditions was suppressed, to be replaced by Soviet (or, more often, indigenous Shamanistic) practices. Nor did World War II bring any noticeable respite, for Buddhism, unlike the other religions of the USSR, was not encouraged to add its voice in support of the war effort. On the contrary, because of deep suspicions of the loyalties of the Buddhist minorities due to Japanese efforts to woo the Mongolian peoples, the Soviet Buddhist nationalities experienced additional hostility, and suffered such crippling disabilities as large-scale population transfers and intensive police and investigatory pressures throughout the war. By the end of the war Buddhism in the USSR was decimated, maintaining a furtive, all but invisible existence in private practices and habits among the people individually. The institutional base of Buddhism has not been extensively rebuilt since that time, and thus Soviet foreign policy has very little on which to build a Buddhist component in international relations. If problems of credibility arise due to the truncated domestic base remaining to Islam (and even, to a lesser degree, to Orthodoxy), these problems are almost insuperable in so far as Buddhists are concerned.

To compensate for this reduced domestic base, Soviet foreign policy has sought wherever possible to develop subsidiary facilities for international relations with Buddhists. The Mongolian People's Republic would be the natural ally in this regard, for Mongolia is a Buddhist country which, although technically independent politically, is firmly established within the Soviet orbit. Unfortunately, institutional Buddhism in Mongolia is only moderately better off than in the USSR, for during the inter-war period practitioners of Soviet atheism were only too successful in the bitter struggle to eradicate Buddhism from Mongolian society, a struggle waged with such intensity that on occasion tanks were used to overcome the religious demands of the population. As a result, Mongolian Buddhism, while helpful, suffers from limitations due to its eroded domestic base similar to those from which Soviet Buddhists suffer. Nevertheless, Mongolian lamas are represented on the Mongol Peace Committee and the Mongol Committee for Afro-Asian Solidarity, and contribute their voices to Soviet international propaganda in outspoken terms.[54] Thus Mongolian Buddhists reacted to the Tibetan uprising in 1959 as follows:

Being incited by crafty foreigners, the black forces of reaction and obscurantism have committed bloody crimes and thus plunged the peaceful laymen and innocent clerics in the country in sorrow and sufferings . . . The loathsome rabble and the wretched traitors, having the support of American grabbers, and in collusion with the Chiang clique, attempted to wrest Tibet from People's China, mighty with its national unity.[55]

Similarly, Mongolian Buddhists have added their voices to the protests concerning US involvement in Vietnam.[56]

Some small degree of aid has been elicited from Eastern Europe. According to the journal of the World Fellowship of Buddhists,

Dr. Karel Werner is a leader of a small group of people in Czechoslovakia. His group consists of a number of people with Buddhist interests. Formerly, under the strict regime it was impossible for him to work under a Buddhist name. Recently, under the new liberal government, he was able to found the first Buddhist organization under the name of ' The Buddhist Circle of Brno '. He was invited by Buddhists in England to visit them there. But just before he was due to leave the blow fell. It was obvious that such a religious activity is diametrically opposite to the Russian Communists.[57]

Nevertheless, the WFB maintains a Regional Centre in Prague, which was represented (by proxy) at its 9th General Conference in 1969.[58] Buddhism in Hungary, building upon the sporadic interest of individuals from the region since the early nineteenth century, has a rather curious recent history. In 1951 a Buddhist Mission was founded by Ernö Hetényi-Heidlberg, which merged with the Eastern European branch of the Arya Maitreya Mandala (AMM), whose headquarters were established in Budapest. In 1956 Hetényi founded a small seminary, which by 1959 claimed nearly 500 followers and was receiving a small monthly cash donation from India. Apparently this centre was not able to elicit universal respect; according to Russell Webb:

The past history of Hetényi will perhaps explain this. During all the time he has claimed to be a Buddhist—since before the War—he has been a professional night club dancer, newspaper reporter, and uniformed officer of the notorious *A. V. O.* (*Allam Vedelmi Osztaly*—'State Protecting Department'—a euphemism for the Hungarian Communist Gestapo!). He has been well-known in occult circles but is undoubtedly still an *A. V. O.* agent nominated by the State to report on those interested in Oriental matters; he is reputed to be a police informer and to have been responsible for the imprisonment of fellow citizens. Aged about 56, not actively employed now, Hetényi lives with his mother, second and fourth wives (the latter, a very attractive, mini-skirted girl in her early twenties) in a large apartment which has the rare privilege of possessing a private telephone.[59]

In 1967, a new Buddhist organization, the Maha Bodhi Society, was formed in Budapest, apparently by former members of the AMM, which was accepted by the WFB as a Regional Centre in 1969, even though it had not yet secured the recognition of the Hungarian State.[60]

Soviet scholarship on Buddhism has developed remarkably since the mid-1950s, and to some degree it has been able to be of service in foreign relations. In large measure, this is due to a happy conjunction of Soviet possession of archival materials of considerable rarity (recovered from Soviet Asia) and the detached, philosophical interests which are often evident in Buddhist countries. In some instances a common scholarly interest has proved able to serve in lieu of a common religious conviction, and Buddhists from abroad have been favourably impressed with Soviet Buddhist studies.[61] Soviet scholarship received a considerable windfall in 1959 with the decision of Iurii N. Rerikh to return from India to the land of his father, and the special sector for study of the religion and philosophy of ancient India which he founded in the Asian People's Institute of the Academy of Sciences survived his untimely death in 1961 and continues the study of Buddhism.[62]

Direct Buddhist participation in Soviet foreign policy has been relatively infrequent. During the early fifties Buddhists on occasion added their voices to the various peace meetings held within the USSR, and were sent on occasional trips domestically for propaganda purposes.[63] In 1955 the Chief Lama was brought to Moscow for a meeting with the Prime Minister of Burma, U Nu, who was by no means a disciple of things Soviet.[64] In 1950 he had declared in connection with the formation of the Burmese Buddha Sasana Council:

Some even go to the extent of declaring that Lord Buddha was a lesser man than Karl Marx. It will be one of the functions of this Buddhist organization to combat such challenges in the intellectual field. . . If any Marxist comes out with the statement that Karl Marx was a very wise man, it is not our concern to question it. But if he encroaches on our sphere and ridicules Lord Buddha whom we all adore and revere and if he has the effrontery to say that Marx was wiser than Lord Buddha, it is up to us to retaliate. It will be our duty to retort in no uncertain terms that the wisdom or knowledge that might be attributed to Karl Marx is less than one-tenth of a particle of dust that lies at the feet of our great Lord Buddha.[65]

Apparently the Chief Lama's attempts to persuade U Nu were not entirely successful, for during the latter part of his reign Burma began to lean slightly more to the West. With the military *coup d'état* in 1962, relations between Burmese and Soviet Buddhists were effectively terminated, for the Ne Win government has applied a policy of reducing potentially partisan foreign contacts to the minimum.

In 1956 some publicity for foreign consumption was released in connection with the celebrations of the 2,500th anniversary of the Buddha's birth, and the following year the newly elected Bandido Hambo Lama, Eshi-Derji Sharapov, attended a meeting of the World Peace Council in Ceylon. In 1958 he entertained a Ceylonese Buddhist monk and Lenin Prize laureate at his headquarters in Ivolga, and in 1959 he was summoned to Moscow for conversations with the Ceylonese ambassador.[66]

During the sixties Soviet Buddhists concentrated the bulk of their efforts on seeking to influence the World Fellowship of Buddhists. The WFB was founded by G. P. Malalasekera of Ceylon in 1950,[67] and as early as in 1956 a Soviet delegation attended the Fourth Buddhist World Conference in Katmandu, and visited India thereafter. The large Soviet delegation to the Sixth WFB Conference in Phnom Penh, Cambodia, in 1961, elicited some negative response because of their intransigence on political questions, and enjoyed little success in affecting the Conference resolutions. At the Eighth Conference in 1967, similar hostility was apparent. There was Soviet representation at WFB meetings throughout the sixties, with the possible exception of the meeting at Chengmai, Thailand, when S. D. Dylykov was detained in India, having failed to secure a visa. At the Ninth Conference in Malaysia in 1969, representatives of Soviet Buddhism played a conspicuous role; Dylykov, a Professor at the Academy of Sciences in Moscow, was elected one of the twelve WFB Vice-Presidents, thereby eclipsing the Bandido Hambo Lama and the Did Hambo Lama, both of whom were also in the Soviet delegation. During the conference Dylykov served as the Vice-Chairman of the First Plenary Session and Chairman of the Second, and he and the two chief lamas were among the twelve members of the Humanitarian Committee, while two other Soviet Buddhists served on the nine-member Finance Committee. The latter, acting on a Soviet proposal, recommended that Regional Centres be invited to provide salaries for Under-Secretaries to assist in the work of the WFB.[68] The WFB maintains a Regional Centre in the USSR, under the directorship of Dylykov, with its headquarters at the Asian Peoples' Institute in the Moscow Academy of Sciences.[69] Thus Soviet Buddhism enjoys the unique distinction of having the only religious institution operating under the aegis, and with the facilities, of a State-supported enterprise, and if the aims of the WFB (such as ' to propagate the sublime doctrine of the Buddha ') are in conflict with the avowedly atheistic and antireligious goals of the Academy of Sciences, apparently this radical contradiction in terms has not yet occasioned disharmony.

Despite more than a decade of intensive effort, Soviet attempts to influence the political tendencies of the WFB have not enjoyed any remarkable success. The Vietnamese War has, if anything, induced a greater inclination towards the West in the WFB due to the apprehensions felt among Thai, Cambodian, Taiwanese, South Korean and other members; and opposing sentiments from such delegations as the Soviet and Vietnamese (and, more recently, Ceylonese members) have been receiving diminishing attention. At the close of the sixties, there were signs that Soviet Buddhists were in process of re-evaluating their hitherto almost exclusive concentration on the WFB in international Buddhism.

Late in 1969 it was reported that a meeting in Ulan Bator, Mongolia, was discussing plans for forming a World Socialist Buddhist Sangha Council. (This would correspond roughly to a clerical organization: the WFB includes laymen.) Soviet Buddhists have not participated in the work of the World Buddhist Sangha Council, formed in 1966 with headquarters in Ceylon, and it would appear that the proposed organization would be intended to rival the present Council.[70]

Concurrently, plans were laid for a Meeting of Asian Buddhists to be held at Ulan Bator the following year.[71] M. Sumanatissa, who led the Ceylonese delegation to this planning session, visited Moscow on his way to Ulan Bator, and both he and the delegate from Nepal had been invited to the Zagorsk Conference in 1969. The meeting was held in June 1970, and it is indicative of the failure of Soviet Buddhists to secure complete co-operation from the WFB that the latter sent no delegates to the meeting but was represented merely by an observer.[72] Indeed, the message sent by Princess Poon Pismai Diskul of Thailand, the President of the WFB, was exceedingly cool:

> I would stress the prohibitive element behind this high-sounding and most often repeated practice of *METTA*. This is the absence of prejudice and is the indispensable element... In absolute terms there is no prejudiced *METTA*, or one based on love for one side and hatred against the other.
>
> It is because of this fact that the World Fellowship of Buddhists has so far refused to get involved in the field of politics, which, frankly speaking, cannot be divested of bias or prejudice, siding with the one against the other and extolling one side to the detriment of another.[73]

The proceedings of the meeting seemed much more conformable to Soviet policy positions than WFB sessions have been. Indeed, the meeting was marked by a level of polemic reminiscent of the salad days of the peace campaigns twenty years previously. The Chief Lama of Mongolian Buddhists, S. Gombojav, declared in his report:

> World reactionary forces headed by American imperialists are stubbornly coming out against the efforts of peace champions demanding universal disarmament; they are deliberately aggravating the international situation, threatening with a new world war.
>
> It is a vivid manifestation of the dark schemes of the reactionary forces thirsting for bloodshed, of their plans to delay social development, to retain the unjust order of exploitation of man by man: to retain their pressure to bear upon the dependent countries.

. . . .

> By expanding and escalating this war in Indo-China, and creating a serious threat to Asian peoples and international peace and security, American imperialists are committing all sorts of sins in the three aspects, body, speech and mind. American warmongers have destroyed valuable historical monuments of ancient Buddhist culture and art, unique on earth, and killed thousands of Buddhists.[74]

The Venerable K. Mahanama of Ceylon was no less outspoken:

> The US has resorted to a naked and terrifying militarism surpassing in its brutality even the worst that Hitler and his lords were capable of conjuring up even during moments of the wildest frenzy.

. . . .

Houses are dynamited with the inmates locked inside. On many occasions pregnant mothers have been lined up and their bellies ripped open by bayonets followed by the loud guffaws of their murderers for having managed to kill some Vietcong even before they were born. Very often young women and girls are herded into groups to be raped over and over again and the majority of them die in the process. The survivors are done to death summarily.

Whenever toddlers survived a general massacre their heads are bashed in with the butt ends of rifles in the style of getting rid of some irritating vermin. The most barbarous forms of torture are also used, and there have been numerous cases of men and women being impaled . . .

.   .   .   .

. . . The result is that prostitution and all kinds of sexual vices have become the most outstanding features of normal day to day life in these areas.

Hand in hand with these developments, pimping has become a highly developed and lucrative profession, and even boys and girls in their early teens whose physical assets are not attractive enough to be of any service to the US soldiers and the local debauchees have taken to it in a large way. At the same time gambling, night-club orgies, blue film centers, and the most revolting forms of naked shows, all of which are a downright insult to traditional morals, have reached a very high level of social acceptance.[75]

The various resolutions and appeals issued by the meeting, while perhaps less vivid, were outspoken and exceedingly resolute in condemning American imperialism, particularly concerning Vietnam, and were in all respects compatible with the requirements of Soviet foreign policy.[76]

The participants unanimously decided to establish a continuing Committee for Promoting Co-operation of Asian Buddhists for Peace, with Gombojav as President, Sumanatissa of Ceylon and N. Jinaratana of India as Vice-Presidents, and M. Jugder of the Mongolian People's Republic as Secretary-General.[77] In view of this action, together with Soviet Buddhist representation at the World Conference on Religion and Peace at Kyoto, Japan, the following October (where, it should be noted, their participation bore none of the marks of outspokenness characteristic of the Ulan Bator meeting), it would appear that Soviet Buddhists are in process of revising their previous concentration on the WFB and are exploring new avenues of rendering service to Soviet foreign policy.

Thus Buddhists from the USSR, who have enjoyed relatively few opportunities for co-operation in Soviet foreign affairs, seem to be entering a period of increasing international activities. In view of the growing emphasis on the Third World in Soviet foreign policy, the role of Buddhism holds promise of considerable expansion, with, perhaps, corresponding increases in effectiveness in Buddhist areas of the world.

7   The East-West Confrontation

THE primary determinant in Soviet foreign policy considerations is, of course, the non-Communist West. For all its intense activity among the uncommitted nations, the USSR maintains an acute awareness that it is the power of the industrially and technologically developed world which defines the parameters and sets the limits of its conduct of foreign affairs. Strategically, it is the nuclear stalemate which establishes the maxima of achievements which may be sought in foreign affairs. Militarily, it is the relative balance of force, and the degree to which it may be effectively employed, which determines the limits of action in a particular locale. Economically, it is the vast and seemingly inexhaustible depth and breadth of Western resources which poses the problems inherent in any design to extend Soviet influence. For all these reasons, and many more, the ultimate focus of Soviet foreign policy has always been, and remains, the confrontation with the West.

The West is the natural field for a religious contribution to Soviet foreign policy. The common historical tradition has assured that Europe and North America are Christian in their religious orientation, and each of the Western nations maintains structures of organized Church life which are influential in most areas of life to a greater or lesser degree. The fact that the Soviet-aligned countries, by and large, share this common Judaeo-Christian heritage provides a natural basis on which mutual concerns may be founded and a degree of influence may be exerted. Soviet foreign policy in the post-war era has not been blind to such potentials in its competition and confrontation with the West.

The activities of the Churches of the USSR and Eastern Europe have been vigorous and wide ranging in East-West international affairs. An immense variety of relations has been established in the Churches' conduct of affairs in the West, with activities, some of them exceedingly complex, conducted on bilateral as well as multilateral bases. Even to catalogue these activities, involving an inexhaustible number of permutations between specific denominations in various individual countries, between groups of similar religious institutions, national and multinational, and among entire divisions of Christianity on national, regional or world-wide scales, would be a complex and extended task far exceeding the scope of the present survey. Instead, an illustrative approach will be taken to the problem of the role of the Churches in the East-West confrontation, concentrating on certain of the specific types of benefits which can accrue to Soviet foreign policy interests from the interaction of Eastern Churches with the West.

The most basic of all services which Eastern Churches can render to their country is to assist in the image-building process. With the post-Stalin awareness of the importance of public opinion, the USSR has devoted much attention to creating a favourable impression among Western people, undertaking tourist, cultural and student exchanges, allocating huge resources to mass media, and engaging in numerous and extensive operations whose sole purpose is to enhance the country's image in the West. Because of natural religious affinities and sympathies, the Churches have been able to render valuable assistance in replacing the popular hostility towards Russia of the Stalin period with a degree of friendliness and openness in the West.

A convenient illustration of this process may be found in the relations of the Russian Baptist Church with the Baptist World Alliance, an international fellowship embracing the millions of Baptists throughout the world. During Stalin's reign Russian Baptists were not represented at BWA functions, and outspoken censure was common. In 1950, for example, the eminent Baptist leader W. O. Lewis proclaimed that in the USSR

there is a certain amount of toleration but no real freedom. At present the Russian state seeks to use the churches for its own purpose. Many ministers of religion have been ' liquidated '. When ministers of religion are imprisoned or banished, the Soviet Government never admits this is because they are preachers. Some trumped-up charge is made against them . . .[1]

Immediately after the death of Stalin measures were taken to overcome this hostility, replacing it with a more desirable picture of Soviet treatment of religion. Russian Baptists began to take an active part in BWA affairs, and enjoyed much success in eliciting sympathy and respect from their fellow believers in the West. Outright condemnation quickly became a rarity in BWA proceedings, and instead the organization came to be infused with a revised evaluation of the USSR, an attitude of tolerance and suspended judgement towards the Russian Churches which, with commendable loyalty towards their country, were working vigorously and harmoniously under conditions which, if difficult and sometimes less than just, were not, after all, inhuman or unprecedented.

On two occasions students from the USSR were allowed to study in Baptist theological schools in Great Britain; their chief function, so far as State interests were concerned, was to solidify and enhance favourable attitudes towards the USSR in Baptist circles. In 1956 five students were studying in two Baptist colleges in England, and one of the students, Michael Zhidkov, was thereafter to be one of the Russian Baptists' most competent and widely respected representatives in international Baptist affairs. A decade later three more Baptists were pursuing theological studies in England.[2]

Success in transforming the image of the USSR in the BWA was great, but not unalloyed. The ' Siberian Christian ' episode provides an instance of a degree of failure in the attempt to build an image sufficiently favourable as to preclude public criticism of Soviet religious policies. In January 1963 thirty-two Christians from Siberia unexpectedly presented themselves at the American embassy in Moscow, asking for political asylum from religious persecution. Asylum was not granted, and, after several hours, the American embassy allowed the Soviet government to take the petitioners into its charge. Because the Siberian Christians claimed to be ' Evangelical Christians ' (which in Russian parlance can denote Baptists generically, Pentecostals or, most probably, Baptistic worshippers who have been denied permission to operate under the auspicies of the legalized Russian Baptist denomination) this episode exercised Baptists in the West considerably, and the Baptist World Alliance issued an immediate protest to Dean Rusk, the US Secretary of State, which contributed somewhat to the unfavourable publicity suffered by the Soviet State in the incident.[3]

In contrast, considerable success was achieved with regard to the schism among Russian Baptists which occurred in the sixties.[4] Because of radically increased State pressure, in 1962 a protest movement, known as the *Initsiativniki*, developed among Russian Baptists, and quickly grew to immense proportions, able to make a serious challenge to the denominational leadership in the USSR. Strong protests were issued in great abundance by the *Initsiativniki*, decrying the allegedly supine acceptance of State interference by the Baptist leadership, and demanding of the State that it terminate its unjust policies and abide by its own laws on religion. Many of these protests reached the West, but, if they found their way into BWA circles, no mention of this development was forthcoming from the BWA until 1966, when the Soviet press finally brought the schism into the open and subjected it to concerted attack. As the affair became known in the West, the BWA began to take note of it in official statements. Thereafter the BWA maintained a continued awareness of the problem, although taking great care in its official utterances to give all due consideration to the evaluations made by the non-schismatic, State-sanctioned Russian Baptist organization which was a member of the BWA. The matter did not become a *cause célèbre* in Baptist circles, and publicity damaging to the image of the Soviet State as guardian of its subjects' freedom of conscience was held to a relatively low level. In this regard, Russian Baptist participation in BWA was almost certainly instrumental in preserving the public image of the USSR in a situation which might otherwise have resulted in much unfavourable publicity.

Russian participation in the Baptist World Alliance provides only an illustration, and a secondary one at that, of the extensive services which the Churches have been able to render in augmenting a favourable image of the USSR in the West. The Prague Christian Peace Conference enjoyed immense success in the image-building process; indeed, it was almost certainly the CPC's ability to elicit and encourage friendly, open attitude towards the USSR that was the basis for its success in rendering more specifically focused services to the State, and which, in the long run, probably will prove to be the most enduring service the CPC was able to render to Soviet foreign policy. Similarly, creating a favourable impression has been the primary—and often the sole—motivation of the State in permitting and encouraging the Churches to undertake a vast range of other activities in the West.

In nearly every respect, the attempt to build a favourable image through Church activity in international affairs must be accounted as an immense success. There have been reversals, to be sure, but the Churches even in the most dismaying of circumstances have been able to mitigate critical reactions in the West, and, in the great majority of the cases, an enduring and important degree of warmth and sympathy has been established. If the general hostility of the cold war has been superseded by a more favourable image of the USSR in Western public opinion, the services of the Church must be given a share of the credit.

Closely allied to the image-building process is a more defensive service which the Churches of the USSR can render to Soviet foreign policy—preventing an unfavourable picture from developing. With rare exceptions, representatives of the Russian Churches have supported their country's official claims of religious toleration, and the result has been the continuation of a degree of ignorance among Western Christians concerning the actual religious situation in the USSR.

Concurrently with the consolidation of Khrushchev's power, the Soviet regime initiated a serious attack against religion on all fronts of domestic life. By 1960 the antireligious campaign had become general, with immense efforts devoted to the propaganda of atheism, and a broad range of restrictions applied in an effective effort to narrow the sphere of religious activity within the USSR. Expulsion from Party organs and educational institutions, loss of jobs and employment discrimination, forcible separation of children from believing parents, interrogation, arrest, imprisonment, and, in a few cases, death were only the severest of a seemingly limitless array of pressures applied against religious believers. Mass closure of Churches took place in the early sixties, and by the fall of Khrushchev late in 1964 the Russian Orthodox Church had been reduced from approximately 16,000 active parishes in the fifties to 7,500,[5] with all other religious denominations suffering proportional, or greater, losses.

Incongruously, it was during this same period that the international activities of the Churches increased dramatically. One of the chief services which the Churches were able to render to the State in such activities was to prevent, or at least delay, Western awareness of the scope and intensity of the antireligious measures being employed within the country, thereby reducing the danger of an outcry in the West such as had arisen during similar periods of pressure against the Churches before the war. Numerous illustrations of such attempts to avoid an adverse reaction in the West are available.

In March 1964 a meeting protesting against religious injustice in the USSR was organized in Paris, and a committee was formed under the nominal leadership of the eminent François Mauriac to inform the West concerning religion in the USSR.[6] At the time, the French government was in process of revising its alignment in a manner which eventually would occasion grave dislocations in the Western alliance, and, in particular, would result in French withdrawal of military support from the North Atlantic Treaty Organization, placing NATO itself in a dubious position. For any widespread protest against treatment of religion in the USSR to arise would have been highly detrimental to the interests of Soviet foreign policy. Metropolitan Nikodim was quick to issue vigorous denials of the veracity of the charges made at the Paris meeting.[7] The focus of these charges had been a number of documents which had reached the West concerning State pressure against the Pochayev Monastery in the USSR, and directly after the rise of protest the Soviet regime abandoned plans to force the monastery's closure, and, indeed, foreign visitors were subsequently brought to Pochayev to observe its continued functioning for themselves.

The *Initsiativniki* affair among the Baptists provided an occasion allowing churchmen to render a service in attempting to minimize possible Western reactions to events within the USSR. Prior to 1966 no public mention whatsoever was made of the schism, which by 1963 had assumed great proportions throughout the USSR. Indeed, during this period Russian delegates continued to use the conventional figure of 5,000 to 5,500 churches in the Russian Baptist denomination, thereby ignoring not only the great inroads which the schismatics had made into the legalized denomination, but also the abundant data in the Soviet press concerning closure of Baptist churches; after the schism had become known in the West, the statistics were revised to half the former figure.[8]

In the later sixties, however, Western Baptists became increasingly concerned about the *Initsiativniki*, and more energetic measures were needed to maintain control of the situation. A British student of Soviet religious affairs, Michael Bourdeaux, began serious study of the *Initsiativniki* problem, and sufficient apprehension was engendered to prompt Michael Zhidkov to make a special visit to London and elsewhere in January 1968—immediately before the publication of Bourdeaux's book on the *Initsiativniki*—to ensure that Baptist leaders in the West would be aware in advance of the contrasting interpretation of the official Russian Baptist leadership on the matter.[9]

When a similar protest developed within the Russian Orthodox Church, measures were likewise taken to attempt to minimize its impact in the West. Late in 1965 two Orthodox priests in Moscow, N. Eshliman and G. Yakunin, wrote open letters to Patriarch Aleksii protesting against acceptance of State interference in the internal life of the Church, and to the government protesting against illegal actions taken against the Church.[10] After these letters had reached the West and had received considerable publicity, the Patriarchate suspended the two priests, and Metropolitan Nikodim took measures to ensure that the Patriarch's encyclical on the matter would receive sufficient publicity in the Western Churches.[11]

These examples merely illustrate the service which the Russian Churches are able to render to State interests in inhibiting hostile reactions in the West to policies applied against religion within the USSR. In the entire range of their activities in the West, Russian churchmen have been diligent to uphold the image of religious freedom which the USSR seeks for itself, and the results of their efforts have been highly successful. Such efforts made a signal contribution to the long delay in Western recognition of the change of the policy of relative toleration in the fifties which, late in the decade, was supplanted by radically increased severity against religion, and it was not until the later sixties that any general awareness of the actual situation of the Churches in the USSR arose in the West. The continuing efforts of Soviet churchmen have helped to keep such awareness minimal in the Western religious community. Furthermore, their efforts to counteract specific instances of nascent concern, such as the examples cited above, have thus far enjoyed absolute success in avoiding the rise of massive hostility in the major Western Churches. Services rendered to Soviet foreign policy interests by the Churches in the matter of preventing widespread opposition to Soviet internal religious policies have been extraordinarily successful.

Just how successful these efforts have been may be illustrated by the experience of the USSR with the Jews. Unlike certain of the other religious denominations, Jews in the USSR have not been allowed to conduct international activities, and they possess no central administration which might enable them to render service to Soviet interests abroad. As a result, no means have been available to counteract or temper the concern of the Western Jewish community for their co-religionists in the USSR. The result has been a massive, concerted, and intense campaign against Soviet anti-Semitism throughout the Western world, a protest, originating in the Jewish community, which has created immense difficulties for the conduct of Soviet foreign policy in the West. The protest has been sufficiently powerful to cause some embarrassment to the USSR in nearly every area of endeavour in the West: formal protests have been lodged in the United Nations, heads of Western governments have publicly censured Soviet anti-Semitism, congresses and parliaments have condemned the USSR on these grounds; leading proponents of amity with the USSR, such as the late Bertrand Russell, have raised the question, and even Communist parties in the West, have expressed disapproval of Soviet anti-Semitism. The effective, well-substantiated, and highly publicized campaign of the Western Jewish community has been highly detrimental to the interests of Soviet foreign policy.

No such concern has been expressed within the Christian Churches, many of whose counterparts in the USSR suffer limitations scarcely less crippling than those applied against Soviet Jews. In large measure, of course, the discrepancy is attributable to the greater cohesiveness of the Jewish community, together with a vivid awareness of the results which followed earlier lack of concern in World War II. However, the Soviet Union has not enjoyed the services of Jewish representatives in Western affairs, and that similar difficulties have not arisen among Western Christians may be attributed, at least in some measure, to the services rendered by the Russian Churches to Soviet foreign policy. *134257*

The primary approach utilized by the Churches in their activities in the West is to seek out and encourage points of view in the Western religious community which are more or less compatible with the interests of the Russian churchmen. This endeavour is, of course, common to all human relations, and, in fact, is nothing more than the universal means of building mutual confidence and seeking to persuade others to accept one's own point of view. Successful development of mutual relations requires a willingness to accede to the other's point of view as well, a process of give and take, and in their international relations of the post-Stalin era the Russian Churches have shown a surprising willingness to build such relationships, entering enthusiastically into the process of deferring to the points of view of others on matters of secondary interest in order to achieve a degree of harmony in primary concerns. In their relations with Western Christians, Russian churchmen have displayed a great willingness to tolerate and make allowance for other points of view in a number of theological, social, and even political matters, working together with Western Christians in ways which are quite foreign to their own theology and tradition. As a result, an atmosphere of goodwill has been generated, and, in matters of prime importance to Soviet foreign policy, a corresponding reciprocity can be elicited from Western churchmen.

The Vietnam issue is perhaps the best illustration of this process of finding and encouraging acceptable points of view in Western Christianity by demonstrating a willingness to reciprocate in other issues. The CPC embraced a wide range of theological points of view in its activities, some of them quite foreign to Eastern traditions, and as a result was able to achieve considerable influence in promulgating a particular approach to its primary topic, peace. Throughout the conduct of their activities in the West, the Russian Churches were alert to viewpoints which were not incompatible with their own approach to the Vietnam issue, and such viewpoints were given great encouragement, publicity, and support in the hope of increasing their currency throughout the Western Churches.

Numerous instances of this approach to Western Churches are available, for this careful and effective process of building harmonious mutual relationships was the hallmark of the international activity of the Russian Churches during the sixties. In 1967, for example, US leaders of the Church of the Brethren were invited to visit the Moscow Patriarchate. At the end of their visit a joint communiqué was issued on 8 October which, over the signatures of representatives of both Churches, stated :

Especially with regard to the undeclared war in Vietnam agreement was reached that military activities there should be speedily terminated both for the preservation of the suffering people of this small country and to avert the threat of escalation into an all-destructive war. The USA should quickly end the bombing of North Vietnam, demonstrating by that very act its willingness to restore the peace, and all parties involved should find the path to the most rapid possible resolution of the conflict. The destiny of Vietnam should, finally, be decided by the Vietnamese people themselves.

These deliberations will be continued in more detail on conclusion of the second exchange of visits, when a delegation of the Russian Orthodox Church will be the guests of the Church of the Brethren in November of this year.[12]

The return visit took place from 11 November to 1 December 1967 and in the course of this visit Nikodim was unusually outspoken on the subject of Vietnam. In a speech at Elgin, Illinois, on 16 November he charged :

The escalation of the war brings suffering not only for the peoples of Vietnam, but also for the people of the United States, whose sons are dying in Southeast Asia, offered in sacrifice to the anti-Communist policy. How long will blood flow? we ask. How long will a few citizens of your country delude themselves with the mirage of national prestige? How long will they think that progressive social changes bear danger for the world order? We have the right to raise these questions because the people of our country, who have conquered in revolution, have by the principle of building socialism proclaimed peace between peoples . . .[13]

The joint communiqué signed by representatives of both Churches at the end of the Russian visit may reflect a slight sharpening of disapproval of US involvement in Vietnam when compared with its predecessor of two months earlier :

Although our conversations expressed certain divergences with regard to contemporary arrangements in Vietnam, both sides are convinced that constructive and essential conditions for the establishment of peace are the immediate cessation of the bombing of North Vietnam by the United States, a cease-fire in Vietnam, and the withdrawal of all foreign troops. The Vietnamese people should be allowed full possibility themselves to determine their personal destiny, without any interference from outside. Together we pray for peace for the long-suffering people of Vietnam.[14]

The careful, patient efforts of the Russian Churches to find and encourage appropriate viewpoints in Western Churches, and their willingness to accept small results which over the long term could progressively lead to the desired positions, resulted in great achievements, and the Churches were able to make a successful and important contribution to Soviet interests through this approach. Particularly when compared with efforts of the Stalin period, when the Churches were insistent on absolute agreement and did not have sufficient range to allow toleration of disagreement, in the hope, and as part of the process, of gaining eventual support on the major issues, the Churches in the sixties demonstrated considerable ability in eliciting in the West sentiments which were compatible with the needs of Soviet foreign policy.

The portfolio of the tactics of Soviet foreign policy in the confrontation with the West includes the attempt to foment discord within the Western alliance, and to some small degree the Church has sought to contribute to this encouragement of disunity in the West. The chief illustration of this effort in Church activities is to be found in the treatment of the German question. Particularly in the CPC, considerable efforts were devoted to protesting against real or imagined *revanchist* sentiments in West Germany, the rearmament of the country, and any schemes designed to give it access to atomic weapons. This was a real issue in its own right, for the expansion of German influence from the mid-fifties onwards certainly seemed contrary to the interests of the Soviet State, and lingering memories of the sufferings caused by the Germans during World War II made fear of the Germans a vital factor among the peoples of Eastern Europe and the USSR. This latter factor was also operative in Western Europe, particularly in areas which had twice in a single generation suffered from German use of force. Hence the continual emphasis on this theme in religious circles might be expected to have some small effect in encouraging latent hostilities within the Western European community of nations.

It should be noted, however, that such attempts to incite disunity occupied a relatively small proportion of the Church's energies. Although the German theme was repeated fairly constantly, it was not sufficiently emphasized as to preclude attempts to gain sympathy and influence within West Germany itself. Numerous joint conferences with German churchmen were held, and the Churches of the East devoted no less energy to building useful relations with the Churches of West Germany than they did with other European Churches.[15]

The general Soviet attempt to disrupt the Western alliance enjoyed impressive success during the sixties. The military homogeneity of the fifties was shattered by the withdrawal of French forces from NATO, and the nascent economic integration did not develop so rapidly as might have been feared. As a result, by the end of the decade the USSR was confronted with much less of a unified, integrated adversary in Western Europe than had seemed likely a dozen years earlier. Despite its efforts, however, it would not seem that the Church made any meaningful contribution whatsoever to this progressive disintegration of the Western alliance, and its efforts to exploit such issues as the German question were almost totally without effect in this regard.

A much more pointed service which the Churches may render to the Soviet State is in providing immediate support in times of crisis. The Churches of Eastern Europe have demonstrated a willingness to utilize every possible channel of influence in support of Soviet interests during moments of extreme tension. The most explicit example of this form of service occurred during the Cuban missile crisis of 1962. Almost immediately upon the proclamation of the US blockade of Cuba, when for several days the world seemed closer to nuclear war than it ever has been, *Izvestiia* carried an appeal signed by Patriarch Aleksii and the heads of the other major Christian denominations of the USSR on 25 October:

Christians cannot and do not have the right to pass by the ill-considered steps of the American Government, which can lead to a terrible, destructive war with tragic consequences for all people. We cannot refrain from testifying to the whole world concerning the fact that such measures are a flagrant transgression of Christian doctrine, a great sin before God.

We call the entire Christian world to immediate, decisive protests against the aggressive acts of the Government of the United States of America. Only such general condemnation of the provocative actions of the President of the USA can guard the world from the danger of thermo-nuclear world war.

We call the Government of the United States of America to show prudence in the name of preservation of the entire human world and immediately to cease provocations against Cuba.

We especially address ourselves to the Christians of the United States of America to raise their voice in defense of peace and to demand of their Government renunciation of the policy of threats and force in relation to Cuba.[16]

Concurrently, telegrams were sent by Nikodim to the United Nations, heads of State, and leaders of national and international religious organizations throughout the world.

It seems doubtful that such attempts to exert an immediate influence on governments at times of extreme tension are especially useful. Certainly during times of crisis, national leaders would seem to have sufficient to occupy their attention to preclude their devoting any special consideration to the wishes of an individual foreign Church leader. Whatever value such protests may have in swaying public opinion, it is almost certain that they have no effect whatsoever in influencing governmental actions in times of grave emergency.

Nor would the direct appeals to heads of State have much effect in times of lesser tension. On occasion religious leaders from Eastern Europe and the USSR have attempted to exercise direct influence on the actions of Western governments, but this would not seem to represent a very serious activity. Earlier in 1962, Patriarch Aleksii had protested directly to President Kennedy concerning US resumption of nuclear testing. Expressing his deep grief at the decision, he said ' You are aware of how inhuman is the policy of intimidation which leads to the frightening nuclear armaments tests, and you know also how contrary this is to the commands of Christ, our Saviour.' He went on to note that the US ' resumed its tests at the very moment when many governments are seeking to conclude an agreement on total disarmament.' [17] However, in view of the fact that Aleksii ignored completely the prior resumption of testing by the USSR, it may be questioned whether such a protest was, indeed, designed to exercise any influence at all on the US government, but instead amounted to an exercise in generating publicity unfavourable to the US decision.

Finally, in assessing the role of religion in the Soviet confrontation with the West, it should be noted that certain voices which are somewhat less than friendly to Communism and the Soviet Union have repeatedly suggested that the true function of religious visitors from the USSR is to serve as ' spies ' for their governments. In the technical sense, this would seem to be a rather absurd charge, for the USSR is possessed of a well-developed, eminently successful capability for gathering intelligence in the Western world, and furthermore, the circles in which such churchmen move in the West would not seem to offer any spectacular opportunities for discovering military, diplomatic, industrial, or any other sort of secrets that would be especially interesting to the Soviet State. To suggest that espionage is their major function would betray a rather poorly developed understanding of the complexity of foreign policy in the modern world, for the benefits which can accrue from the services of the Church in gaining influence in the West far outweigh any possible espionage functions which religious leaders might perform in the West.

This is not to suggest that operations of non-ecclesiastical subversion, such as, for example, attempting to exert pressure on Russian émigrés, are necessarily precluded to representatives of the Church. Metropolitan Nikolai apparently performed such a mission for the MVD in Vienna in the fifties,[18] and in the sixties the US Department of State denied a re-entry visa to the permanent secretary of the Exarch of the Moscow Patriarchate in New York on grounds of activities inconsonant with his position as a churchman. Otherwise, however, there is little or no evidence available to support the charge that Soviet churchmen act as ' spies ' in the West, and, indeed, the known activities of such leaders have been so extremely circumspect as to suggest that traditional espionage and subversion occupy a very small place in the hierarchy of services which the Churches render to Soviet foreign policy.

In summary, the Churches have been able to contribute an important addition to Soviet activities in the East-West confrontation. Particularly in building a favourable image for the USSR, in preventing or inhibiting adverse reactions to domestic religious policies, and in encouraging, strengthening, and influencing points of view in the West which are compatible with the interests of Soviet foreign policy, the Churches have rendered an important service, marginal perhaps, but sufficiently influential to be of concrete benefit in the Soviet confrontation with the West.

One further phenomenon of the East-West confrontation should be mentioned, although it does not form a part of the international activities of the Churches of the East nor, really, is it of more than tangential relevance to Soviet foreign policy. The Christian-Marxist Dialogue represents somewhat of a curiosity in the East-West confrontation, contributing, if anything, little more than mystified embarrassment to the practitioners of Soviet foreign policy.

In the mid-sixties, the Christian-Marxist Dialogue attracted considerable attention in the Western press. The concept was for Christian theologians and Marxist ideologists to meet in dialogue, suspending their traditional hostility in order to explore the other's philosophy, not in order to proselyte, but in the hope of each side gaining a clearer understanding of its own position in the light of the other's experiences. Certain prominent Marxists were attracted, and a number of such dialogues were held. Particularly among Western Christians, the Christian-Marxist Dialogue seemed immensely promising, eliciting great enthusiasm in the Western Church during the latter half of the decade.

However, the concept never realized its potential, for the difficulty of attracting Communists to the dialogues proved insuperable. Such Communists as did respond to the idea with interest were scarcely representative, and, indeed, seemed curiously prone to loss of favour with their parties. Robert Havemann was expelled from the East German Communist Party, and Adam Schaff was expelled from the Polish Party. Erika Kadlecova achieved great prominence in Czechoslovakia during the brief liberalization of 1968, but with the invasion her Party career was abruptly terminated. When Roger Garaudy, who had been the chief Communist proponent of the dialogue, was expelled from the Central Committee of the French Communist Party in 1970, it appeared that almost no one was left to represent the Communist side of the Christian-Marxist Dialogue.

Generally of course, people in the USSR were sublimely uninterested in the whole idea. Russian churchmen denounced it vigorously, while the practitioners of State policy seemed quite content to entrust religious activities to the churchmen. The entire concept of a Christian-Marxist Dialogue doubtless seemed a strange and curious aberration to the practical, efficient, and un-philosophical executors of Soviet foreign policy.

8 Rome and the Orthodox World

ONE of the significant new departures in the contemporary foreign affairs of the Russian Orthodox Church is the tentative exploration of possibilities for *rapprochement* with the Roman Catholic Church. Closer relations with the Vatican would be of great significance for Soviet foreign policy for many reasons. The situation in South America has already been mentioned: in view of Catholicism's dominance in the Latin American countries, any reversal of traditional Catholic antipathy towards Communism offers immense opportunities for extension of Soviet influence there. Perhaps more important is the large role which Catholicism plays in parts of Eastern Europe. In Poland the Catholic Church remains almost a ' state within the State ', and the best energies of the party and government have not resulted in a diminution of the Church's influence over the people, but just the opposite. The resurgence of Catholicism during the brief liberalization in Czechoslovakia gave vivid illustration to the inability of even the most Draconian of measures, applied over an extended period of time, to render the Catholic Church impotent. In Hungary Catholicism remains strong. In the USSR itself, Byzantine Rite, or Uniate, Catholic sentiments have refused to disappear in the western regions of the country even after two decades of complete suppression. Hence any *rapprochement* with the Vatican offers considerable benefits to the Soviet State in its continuing problem of maintaining control in its own domains. In addition, if closer relations could promise an opportunity to influence the Catholic Church to temper its traditional hostility towards Communism, the immense ability of the Church to mould public opinion throughout the world might be of incalculable benefit to Soviet foreign policy interests.

Rapprochement with Rome is beset with manifold problems, however. The centuries of ecclesiastical hostility since the Great Schism of 1054 must somehow be undone or overcome. In addition, the history of Catholic attitudes toward the Soviet State presents numerous difficulties for establishing closer relations in the present world.

The attitude of the Vatican towards the Bolshevik Revolution was somewhat ambivalent. There was some initial exploration of the possibility of whether the fall of the monarchy, which ended Orthodoxy's privileged status, and the obvious need of the Bolsheviks to reduce the power of the Russian Church in the new society, might not present Rome with an opportunity to extend its ministry to the Russian people. Not even the conviction of two Catholic leaders, Cieplak and Budkiewicz (and the latter's execution), could dash such hopes, and although the Pope protested vigorously against Patriarch Tikhon's arrest in 1922, rumours concerning Vatican designs on Russia persisted.[1]

With the waning of the twenties reaction set in, and thereafter relations between the Vatican and the Kremlin became a contest of reciprocal hostility. Rome raised massive and effective protests against persecution of religion in Russia, and the Soviet State reciprocated with unrestrained propaganda against the Catholic Church.[2] At the end of World War II there was a spate of rumours, apparently quite unfounded, about an impending concordat, but it soon became obvious that the hostility was still alive.[3] Pope Pius XII excommunicated the Communists and their collaborators, while in the USSR invective against the Vatican remained a staple of Soviet propaganda, domestic and foreign, throughout the cold war. It was only with the transformation of Soviet foreign policy after the death of Stalin, and with the election of a new Pope, that tentative signs of relaxation began to appear.

It was the primacy of John XXIII which served to initiate the thaw. A dynamic Pope with great vigour and personal magnetism, John displayed little patience with unthinking conservatism in the Church, and devoted himself to the difficult process, considered long overdue in some Catholic circles, of renewal, of transforming the Church in the light of modern times. Along with traditional antipathy towards innovation, the Vatican's habitual, blanket condemnation of Communism was abandoned in favour of a more charitable attitude. The USSR, for its part, was quick to welcome this transformation, with Khrushchev himself expressing appreciation of the Pope's new approach to the changes in the modern world,[4] and with the encyclical *Pacem in Terris* receiving widespread, continuing, and eminently favourable publicity in the Soviet press.

This transformation of attitudes was soon reflected in the Russian Orthodox Church. Hitherto the Church's approach towards the Vatican had reflected almost absolute consistency with the attitude of the State, and propaganda against Rome had received great emphasis, both in the publications of the Church and in its conduct of international affairs.

Prior to the convocation of the Second Vatican Council, at a pan-Orthodox consultation at Rhodes in 1962, in which the Moscow Patriarchate played a vigorous role,[5] it had been agreed that the Orthodox Churches would not send observers to this event. Immediately before the Council, however, Mgr Willibrands, who eventually would succeed to leadership of the Secretariat for Christian Unity, visited Moscow,[6] and when Vatican II opened, two observers from the Moscow Patriarchate, the priest Vitalii Borovoy and the monk Vladimir Kotlyarov, were in attendance.[7] Much favourable publicity resulted, for the Russian Church thus became the only Orthodox Church to be represented at the Council.

Explorations continued for the remainder of Khrushchev's reign. Apparently as a result of an agreement reached privately during Vatican II, the Soviet State made the unusual concession of releasing the long-imprisoned leader of the Uniate Church, Metropolitan Slipiy, who arrived in Rome early in 1963.[8] The precedent of official hostility was broken when the son-in-law of Khrushchev, then the editor of *Pravda*, made a cordial visit to the Pope.[9]

A degree of ambiguity remained in the attitude of the Russian Church towards Rome, however. Cardinal Heenan of Great Britain was invited to Moscow in December 1964 [10] and the following February, Nikodim expressed full support for the dialogue with Rome.[11] However, initiatives taken by the Ecumenical Patriarch, Athenagoras, complicated the picture for the Moscow Patriarchate. As will become evident below, the Russian Church was contemplating a resumption of the competition for primacy in the Orthodox world; thus any dramatic initiatives taken by Patriarch Athenagoras in Istanbul were, at best, a mixed blessing for the interests of the Moscow Patriarchate. In January 1964 for example, Patriarch Aleksii expressed guarded approval of the meeting between Pope Paul VI and Patriarch Athenagoras in Jerusalem, taking care to emphasize, however, that any actions taken by the Ecumenical Patriarch are of significance for his Church alone, and do not necessarily have any relevance for other Orthodox Churches.[12] Two years later Nikodim reiterated this position, stating in a TASS interview that the Ecumenical Patriarch's withdrawal of the ancient anathemas against Rome did not necessarily represent the entire body of Orthodoxy.[13]

After a brief hiatus following the fall of Khrushchev, the search for *rapprochement* was resumed with increasing vigour. In 1967, the President of the USSR, Podgorny, on an official visit to Italy, visited the Pope.[14] This event attracted great publicity, for it marked the first instance in history of direct, personal contact between the government of the USSR and the Pope, who not only is the High Priest of the Roman Catholic Church, but also is the head of the Vatican State. Contacts between Rome and the Russian Orthodox Church accelerated rapidly. In December 1967 Willibrands was invited to Moscow by Patriarch Aleksii for theological discussions, which were 'frank and cordial'.[15] Nikodim reciprocated by visiting Rome in October 1969 when he presented Willibrands with a medal from the Moscow Patriarchate.[16] In 1969 and 1970 consultations were held with US Catholics.[17] In 1968 an earlier controversy was laid to rest when two Russian priests began a two-year course of graduate theological studies at the Collegium Russicum in Rome, which had long been considered by the USSR as an agency for preparing 'Vatican spies' for espionage in Russia.

This movement towards *rapprochement* was by no means confined to the foreign activities of the Russian Orthodox Church. Increasingly vigorous relations with Rome, especially in the later sixties, were initiated both by the Church and by the State in Catholic areas of Eastern Europe (Poland, Hungary, Czechoslovakia), with many exchanges of visits and a number of agreements between the two sides on limited or extensive aspects of political as well as religious relations. The policy of hostility was a thing of the past in Rome, and, for their parts, both the Eastern European Churches and the Communist governments seemed eager to explore all possibilities for promoting greater harmony with Rome.

Inter-Orthodox relations, on the other hand, have not been marked by quite so consistent a search for harmony. While advances have been made in the effort to increase the unity of the Orthodox family of Churches, certain tensions have arisen in the relations of the Moscow Patriarchate with some of its sister Churches.

The inauguration of a pan-Orthodox movement was of great significance in the recent history of Orthodoxy. Numerous inconsistencies of practice, differences of opinion, and jurisdictional controversies had arisen between the various national Orthodox Churches in the twelve centuries since the last Ecumenical Council, and some attempt to overcome such discrepancies was long overdue. Accordingly, a series of pan-Orthodox consultations was begun, at which concrete problems could be discussed and a consensus could be sought, in the hope that such meetings might lead to an eventual Eighth Ecumenical Council. The Moscow Patriarchate participated in these pan-Orthodox meetings, making a useful contribution to the search for common answers to the various disputes. However, Russian participation was not completely free of reluctance, no doubt largely due to the tradition of conservatism in doctrine and practice which is a characteristic of the Russian Orthodox Church, but also because the pan-Orthodox movement was widely identified with the great zeal for unity of the Ecumenical Patriarch. As a result, the Moscow Patriarchate was not unwilling to raise occasional, minor obstructions to the movement's conduct.[18]

The Moscow Patriarchate's relations with the Orthodox Churches of the Russian emigration have been far from smooth. Those Churches which have refused to submit to Muscovite leadership and have remained outside the jurisdiction of the Patriarchate represent an unsolved problem which occasions great annoyance, and occasional difficulty, for the Moscow Patriarchate. The chief offender in this regard is the Russian Orthodox Synod Abroad, which continues the traditional hostility to Communism of the pre-war Karlovtsy jurisdiction, periodically making public protests in the West concerning religious conditions in the USSR. The Soviet State regularly attacks this Church in its propaganda, and the Patriarchate shares the State's disdain for this competitor in the West. At the pan-Orthodox meeting in Geneva in 1968, Nikodim referred to a strong protest which the Moscow Patriarchate had made in 1965 to the Ecumenical Patriarchate because one of his bishops, Metropolitan Emilianos, had conducted a joint liturgy with the Synod's Archbishop Antony (as a result of which Emilianos had been disciplined by the Ecumenical Patriarchate), and made a stern demand that all other Orthodox Churches refuse to have anything to do with this Church.[19] The Moscow Patriarchate was also successful in persuading Patriarch Athenagoras to withdraw jurisdictional sanction from the Russian Church in France, occasioning a deep crisis within the émigré community there.[20] In May 1967 Aleksii sent a telegram to Athenagoras warning him to avoid all contact with representatives of the Russian Orthodox Metropolia of America during their projected visit to the Middle East, and three months later lodged a bitter protest over the presence of bishops of the Ecumenical Patriarchate at the ordination of a bishop of the US Metropolia.[21]

These various difficulties with the diaspora in the emigration would appear to be a special problem of the Russian Orthodox Church. By way of contrast, the Armenian Orthodox Patriarch seems to enjoy the best of relations throughout the Armenian emigration, despite the fact that he is a Soviet citizen. A vigorous programme of visits to Echmiadzin, monetary donations to the Mother Church from the emigration, and harmonious interchange of all sorts take place among Armenians scattered throughout the world. In 1963 reconciliation seems to have been achieved with the Armenian Patriarchate of Cilicia, which at one time was quite hostile to the Soviet orientation, when the heads of the two jurisdictions (of whom the Patriarch of Echmiadzin is ' first among equals ') met in Jerusalem.[22]

Apart from, and in many respects in diametrical opposition to, the quest for unity, it is the competition with the Ecumenical Patriarchate which seems to have determined much of the recent policy of the Russian Church in the Orthodox world. During the course of the sixties it became increasingly evident that the desire for pre-eminence in Orthodoxy, which had lain dormant since the failure of the attempted *tour de force* in 1948, was being revived in the conduct of the foreign affairs of the Russian Orthodox Church. The attempt to erode the position of the Ecumenical Patriarch has taken a number of diverse forms, ranging from the minor embarrassment of Moscow's continuing refusal to accede to his wish to pay a fraternal visit returning Aleksii's visit to Istanbul in 1960,[23] to a number of important, and sometimes bold, manoeuvres in the Russian Church's conduct of affairs in the Orthodox world.

As has already been noted, if the Moscow Patriarchate were to attain a position of recognized leadership similar to that now ceded to the Ecumenical Patriarchate throughout the Orthodox world, significant advantages and opportunities would accrue to Soviet foreign policy. More specifically, however, there are political ramifications of the competition for pre-eminence in the Church which are of immediate interest to Soviet foreign policy.

Because of Turkey's strategic importance in the geographic deployment of NATO, and, of course, because of its control of the USSR's only direct access to the Mediterranean, Soviet foreign policy has devoted considerable attention to the courtship of Turkey, seeking to weaken its adherence to the Western alliance. A corollary of this policy is a fairly stern approach to Greece, for this prominent outpost of NATO is an annoyance not only to Soviet designs in the Mediterranean: its common border with the southern perimeter of the Soviet family of nations, together with its perennial—and recently augmented—hostility towards Communism is not particularly welcome from the Soviet point of view. Hence the USSR has pursued a co-ordinated policy in the Aegean of courtship of Turkey and hostility towards Greece.

The Church has an obvious contribution to make to this policy. Turkey has long exhibited an almost xenophobic hostility to its minuscule Orthodox population, and, indeed, so extreme was its antipathy toward the Ecumenical Patriarchate that for a brief period in the mid-sixties it appeared that its expulsion was being contemplated. Hence any tensions generated between the Patriarchates in Moscow and Istanbul may be expected to be welcomed by the Turkish government. Concurrently, any signs of hostility in Church relations between Moscow and Athens will be appreciated in Turkey, while at the same time conforming to the tenor of the Soviet State's policies in the area. Particularly in its relations with Greece, the Moscow Patriarchate has demonstrated a degree of adherence to this general policy scheme.

With regard to the Cyprus dispute, the Moscow Patriarchate firmly supported the resistance to Greek annexation of the island. In this regard, the position of the Russian Church was compatible with that of Turkey, which, because of the large Turkish minority on the island, was vehemently opposed to annexation. On 5 March 1964 Aleksii sent a telegram to Archbishop Makarios, the Chief of State of Cyprus, expressing the ' complete sympathy and solidarity ' of the Russian Orthodox Church ' in the righteous struggle of the people of Cyprus for the freedom, territorial integrity, and sovereign rights ' of Cyprus.[24] Such support, however welcome it may have been to Turkey, would scarcely elicit much gratitude in Greece.

When the monarchy in Greece was replaced by a military government, the Russian Church joined in the not inconsiderable wave of opposition to the new political structure of the country. Aleksii was quick to protest against the enforced retirement of the Archbishop of Athens in 1967.[25] On 2 January 1968 Aleksii sent a telegram to the Greek Primate protesting against the summary arrest and confinement of those whom the military regime considered enemies, among whom were a number of Communists.

Your Grace!

In the days of the Epiphany festivals we have the moral obligation to turn to you with our word of spiritual anxiety concerning those sons and daughters of the Greek people who for their views and aspirations for freedom and democracy have for a long time been unjustly confined in prison. We turn to you with our fraternal exhortation to raise your voice as an Archpastor, which may have its influence, concerning the liberation of all of them from prison and concentration camps, which, doubtless, will serve the establishment of normal life in Greece and will bring joy to all people of good will. Such an address by you would be a gift acceptable to the Lord Jesus, the Savior of the world, Who has placed your spirit for the

liberation of many, ' to proclaim release to the captives . . . to set at liberty those who are oppressed ' (Luke 4 : 18).
  With fraternal love,
    Aleksii, Patriarch of Moscow and All Russia [26]

A fortnight later he sent another telegram protesting at the house arrest of the Metropolitan of Salonika, with similar telegrams dispatched to the Ecumenical Patriarch and the General Secretary of the World Council of Churches, while Metropolitan Filaret, in his capacity as Vice-President of the USSR-Greece Society, issued a similar protest.[27] In May 1969 Aleksii found occasion to protest to the Greek Prime Minister concerning violations of Russian rights and traditions in the monastic community of Mt Athos.[28]

All these actions, which could make a contribution to the hostile publicity concerning the situation in Greece, were not without relevance to the interests of Soviet foreign policy. They contained another dimension, however, which was also beneficial to the aspirations of the Russian Church. Because of common historical and ethnic roots, relations between the Ecumenical Patriarchate and the Greek Orthodox Church are exceedingly close, and, indeed, the latter is one of the Patriarchate's firmest, most powerful supporters in the world of Orthodoxy. Hence by attacking Greece (and, by implication, the Greek Church) the Moscow Patriarchate might hope to have some small effect in contributing to the erosion of the Ecumenical Patriarchate's base of power in inter-Orthodox affairs.

A more overt attempt to alter the balance of power in Orthodoxy took place in the Church of Antioch in Syria in the spring of 1966.[29] At a Synod of bishops convened to elect a successor to the See of Latakia, a group of bishops sympathetic to Moscow attempted to seize power and force the election of a candidate of their choice. When this manoeuvre failed they walked out and organized a rump Synod which proceeded to elect their own Bishop of Latakia. This attempt also failed and the majority elected a more acceptable candidate. The matter was not settled, however, until parishioners had faced a confrontation with Syrian tanks in defending their cathedral, and the new bishop was not allowed entry by the Syrian government but had to rule his diocese *in absentia* from Tripoli, in Lebanon. The entire affair was accompanied by exceedingly high tensions, and for several days the Church of Antioch was in major crisis.

This election was more important than it might appear at first glance. With the sympathies of the episcopate divided, the election of a bishop sympathetic to Moscow might have altered the alignment significantly within the Antiochene episcopate. In view of the advanced age of the Patriarch of Antioch, a successor would have to be elected by the bishops in the foreseeable future, and any increase in Russian sympathies among the eventual electorate would be of immense significance. Obviously, the alignment of the Patriarch of Antioch, one of the Four Ancient Patriarchates, would be of great influence in determining the balance of power in Orthodoxy as a whole.

There is no evidence of direct Russian involvement in the affair. By curious coincidence, however, the incident took place at the same time as the visit of officials of the Russian Orthodox Church to dedicate the cathedral in Damascus and the hospital in Beirut which had been built with funds donated to the Church of Antioch by the Moscow Patriarchate; [30] and after the abortive Latakia *putsch* the Moscow Patriarchate found it expedient finally to accede to requests from Beirut that a replacement be sent for the representative of the Moscow Patriarchate there, Vladimir Kotlyarov, who had elicited considerable unpopularity by his tactless attempts to exercise influence on the local Orthodox. In fact, there seemed all but universal agreement in the local Orthodox population that the Latakia affair had been undertaken, at the very least, with Russian collusion.

At the close of the decade two further manoeuvres were initiated by the Moscow Patriarchate which promised to become of great significance in the attempt to wrest supremacy from the Ecumenical Patriarchate. According to the *New York Times*, Moscow announced a unilateral decision to offer limited intercommunion to Roman Catholics:

The notification from Moscow said the Holy Synod of the Russian Orthodox Church decided last Dec. 16 to allow its clergy in the Soviet Union and abroad to administer the sacraments under certain circumstances to Roman Catholics.

Russian Orthodox priests, therefore, can now perform baptisms or weddings for Roman Catholics, as well as administer Extreme Unction, the Eucharist and Penance.

The action by the Russian Patriarchate, which unilaterally speeds up the process of reunion between the Roman Catholic and the Orthodox churches, caused surprise . . .[31]

A decision of this magnitude would normally demand the advance agreement of all the Orthodox Churches, if not an Ecumenical Council; and even if it were taken by the ' first among equals ' it would be certain to evoke a storm of protest in the other Churches, and charges that he had exceeded his authority. For such a decision to be taken unilaterally by the Moscow Patriarchate was a studied affront, and almost certainly a challenge to the Ecumenical Patriarch and his pre-eminence in Orthodoxy, particularly inasmuch as Athenagoras already had specifically ruled out intercommunion with Roman Catholics, ' since no decision of this kind was ever taken by the Orthodox Church and since intercommunion between the Orthodox Church and the other churches does not as yet exist.' [32]

Concurrently, the Moscow Patriarchate initiated another serious challenge to the Ecumenical Patriarch's authority. In an astonishing reversal of a policy of four decades' standing, Moscow held consultations with the Russian Metropolia in the US and agreed to grant the latter autocephaly. The agreement became effective in 1970.[33] As yet it is difficult to discern the reasons for Moscow's making a concession of such magnitude to the hitherto schismatic Russian Church in America, which envisioned Moscow's closing its Exarchate in New York, surrendering its few parishes in the US to the Metropolia, and recognizing the latter's complete independence. From the point of view of Soviet foreign policy it was not an entirely unreasonable decision, for the generally non-political attitudes of the Metropolia had demonstrated that such an augmentation of its status was most unlikely to threaten or damage Soviet interests, and, furthermore, the maintenance of the Exarchate and its few parishes had required considerable subsidies without any effect whatsoever in furthering Soviet interests among the American people. Finally, there may have been subsidiary benefits in the agreement, such as the change in the status of the Japanese Orthodox Church, which offered some small attraction to the interests of Soviet foreign policy.

With regard to the competition with the Ecumenical Patriarchate, however, the decision represented an immensely serious challenge. As it had done immediately after the war, the Moscow Patriarchate once again was arrogating to itself the traditional right of the Ecumenical Patriarch to grant autocephaly to new national Churches. Furthermore, by granting the Russian Church autocephalous dignity, the Moscow Patriarchate was introducing further complexity into the already confused situation of Orthodoxy in America. Inasmuch as the Ecumenical Patriarchate is heavily dependent on the contributions from its affiliates in America, it could scarcely fail to view this decision by Moscow with the utmost gravity, and, indeed, outspoken protests were quickly forthcoming, including the threat of withholding recognition from the new Church.

Thus by the close of the sixties the Russian Church was moving with increasing boldness towards *rapprochement* with Rome, and in its grave challenges to the supremacy of the Ecumenical Patriarch, towards disunity within Orthodoxy. It seems apparent that the Moscow Patriarchate is not unwilling to entertain the prospect of a possible major realignment within Christendom, a realignment which, *inter alia*, might offer increased opportunities for rendering a service to Soviet foreign policy.

9   The World Council of Churches

FROM the point of view of Soviet foreign policy, the interaction of the Russian Church with the World Council of Churches is by far the most crucial of the international religious activities of the sixties. The membership of the Russian Orthodox Church in the WCC introduced a new dimension, entailing a radical transformation, quantitatively and qualitatively, in the services rendered to Soviet foreign policy by the Church, and ushering in a vast array of new opportunities, problems, and complexities. In large measure, the overall ability of the Church to make an effective contribution to the interests of the Soviet State depended upon the success or failure of its activities in the context of the WCC.

The World Council of Churches is the chief organizational expression of the ecumenical movement, an influential body embracing Christians of nearly every denominational affiliation (with the exception of Roman Catholicism) throughout the world. Its membership is vast, fluid, and complex, representing approximately 200 Churches, affiliations of Churches, and denominational and interdenominational agencies (in fact, the complexity of its membership, ranging from small, minority Churches in particular regions to huge agencies representing a large number of individual Churches, some of them themselves also members of the WCC, precludes any exact, useful enumeration of its membership). As many as 170,000,000 Christians may be represented by the member Churches and organizations of the WCC.

The primary function of the WCC is to serve as a forum for broad discussions, detailed negotiations, and far-reaching dialogue among the various Christian viewpoints represented. In operation, the WCC reflects the complex interplay of the almost infinite array of ideas, pressures, and influences of the fluid and inconstant alliances among the members on the specific points at issue, and if it is difficult for such a large and complex organization to achieve a practical, efficient democracy in the most direct sense of the term, its actions, by and large, faithfully reflect the opinions and desires of the participants in its meetings.

The staff of the WCC is arranged in a most complex fashion, under the leadership of a General Secretary and Central Committee, and with a large number of major and minor departments, commissions, and committees, often with overlapping portfolios. Actual (as opposed to nominal) leadership and control are apportioned between the General Secretary, Associate General Secretaries, Presidents, Departmental officers, interdepartmental committees, and Central and Executive Committees in a manner which, seemingly, defies explanation. Effective leadership in such a staff organization presupposes a high degree of understanding and skill in the employment of that peculiar sort of politics which prevails in religious organizations, and the WCC is possessed of exceedingly great talents for Church leadership within its corps of officers and staff.

Nevertheless, the WCC is quite responsive to the desires of its larger membership, despite the staff's possession of unquestioned skills in the manipulative techniques of normal Church politics. In part this responsiveness is doubtless due to the integrity and commitment of the leadership. In the last analysis, however, it is also due to the fact that whatever the skills of the leadership, ultimate authority does, indeed, reside in the constituency, and only a certain degree of divergence can be tolerated between the desires of the membership and the actual decisions of the leadership; transgression of these boundaries will result inevitably in the alienation of the members, who possess the ultimate power (withholding of support, or even withdrawal from WCC membership) to insist that their views receive adequate representation. Indeed, the financial difficulties which were arising at the close of the decade may reflect, at least in part, a degree of alienation among the rank-and-file due to actions taken by the WCC as an organization which were not of interest to an important portion of the members.

The basic purpose of the World Council of Churches is that of the ecumenical movement as a whole, the search for Christian unity. The logical incongruity of the deep divisions which exist within the Christian Church (many, if not most, of them more or less due to historical circumstances), demands exploration and re-evaluation of whether the common faith does, indeed, necessitate divisions between Christians. The WCC was created as a means for facilitating this search for Christian unity.

From the inception of the ecumenical movement, a deep stream of political implications has been inherent in this search for unity. The ecumenical movement was firmly committed to the ideal that Christians need not and must not be separated by the transient political divisions of the contemporary world. Even before World War II, for example, conversations were held between American and Japanese Christians, dedicated to overcoming fissures in Christian unity caused by divergent political alignments, and immediately after the war extensive aid was given to the Churches of Germany and Japan to heal the wounds caused by the political conflicts of World War II. Throughout its history, the World Council of Churches has been deeply committed to this search for unity despite political divisions between Christians.

In addition, the WCC seeks to make a positive contribution to the contemporary Church, exploring and leading the way in the attempt to find answers to the problems faced by the Church in the modern world. Despite the conservatism of certain of its member Churches, the WCC has not allowed itself to remain shackled by a burden of outworn traditions, particularly in matters relating to society, but on the contrary has cultivated an openness to progressive innovations seeking to make the faith relevant to the modern world.

The WCC operates under considerable limitations in implementing these goals. It possesses no power or authority over its member churches. It has no means of dictating their actions, but must rely entirely on unimpeachable correctness in its decisions, the eminence and prestige of its reputation and that of its participants, and the goodwill of the member Churches if it is to exercise an effective influence on their actions. It is able to represent their interests in international and interdenominational affairs, but only with their prior, subsequent, and continued consent. Hence, the WCC possesses no means of pretending to structural, ecclesiastical authority in the Christian world—and has little desire for such authority. Its primary function has been, and remains, to provide a forum where Christians can meet together in ecumenical harmony, and can act together on matters of mutual concern.

The WCC does possess, however, great power in influencing public opinion particularly in the West, both within the Churches and in society at large. Its enormous prestige is a powerful force in the modern world. The WCC is by far the most influential voice in the entire Protestant, and, increasingly, Protestant and Orthodox community, of incalculable effect in influencing and determining attitudes throughout the world, and able effectively to mobilize vast publicity concerning, and often largely favourable to, its position on an enormous range of subjects.

Obviously, such an organization as this offers great prospects for Soviet foreign policy-makers in their attempts to further the interests of the USSR throughout the world. The intensity of the desire for Christian unity in the WCC and among its members offers a natural opportunity for warm and effective relations to be established with the Russian Church. The refusal to allow political divisions to separate Christians ensures that, at the very least, the USSR can gain a hearing for its attitudes concerning the major political problems of the times, while the WCC's search for Christian relevance and receptivity to progressive approaches suggests that the hearing received by the interpretations of the USSR may not be altogether hostile. Finally, the vast potential of the WCC for mobilizing public opinion is of immediate relevance for Soviet foreign policy in its desire to increase the influence of the USSR in the contemporary world.

Under Stalin, the Russian Church was profoundly hostile to the ecumenical movement, considering it a heretical attempt by Protestant sectarianism to increase its influence by impermissible means, and, in political terms, regarding it as an arm of capitalist imperialism. At the conference organized by the Moscow Patriarchate in 1948, the Russian spokesmen denounced Orthodox participation in the strongest of terms, because, *inter alia*, ' of the close kinship between œcumenical activity and other contemporary non-Church, political and sometimes secret international movements'.[1] During the conduct of the peace campaign Protestantism as a whole, excepting only those few individuals who collaborated with the work of the World Peace Council, was regularly and roundly condemned.

After Stalin's death the attitude of the Russian Church towards Western Christianity began to change. In 1955 negotiations were resumed between the National Council of Churches in the US and the Moscow Patriarchate, which culminated in an exchange of visits the following year. The American visit to Moscow may have been of some effect in encouraging revision of the approaches used by Russian churchmen in international affairs, for the Americans caused Metropolitan Nikolai a degree of embarrassment by bringing up the issue of specific inaccuracies which had been promulgated by the Russian Church during the peace campaign, and particularly the germ-warfare issue which had been utilized in the propaganda against US involvement in the Korean War.[2] The best answer Nikolai could give was, ' I think that the question refers to such a period of the distant past that it is not useful to discuss. Now we are seeking ways of understanding each other better, of growing closer to each other.'[3] Further evidence of a revised attitude towards Western Christians was given when the Anglicans and Orthodox met in theological conference in Moscow the same year.

Relations with the World Council of Churches were also becoming more friendly. In 1957 Metropolitan Nikolai expressed greetings to the Central Committee of the WCC in the following terms:

We Christians must stand above the political contradictions of our time and give to the divided peoples an example of unity, of peace, of brotherhood and of love, removing ourselves from all self-sufficient isolationism, and of friendly relations to each other.

We Orthodox Christians are in great sympathy with the ecumenical movement because we believe that our Western brothers honestly aim at overcoming the destructive separation in faith.[4]

Relations continued to improve, and fraternal exchanges of messages and visits between the WCC and the Russian Orthodox Church took place with increasing frequency. When Nikolai's career as chief representative of the Moscow Patriarchate in foreign affairs was abruptly terminated and he was replaced by Nikodim, relations continued to improve at an even greater rate.

The climax of the growing *rapprochement* came late in 1961, when the World Council of Churches, meeting in General Assembly in New Delhi, voted overwhelmingly to accept the application of the Russian Orthodox Church for membership in the WCC. This inaugurated a new era in the foreign relations of the Russian Church, enabling it to commence vigorous activity in the ecumenical movement as a full member of the WCC.

The Russian Orthodox Church enjoyed a position of considerable prominence and potential power in the WCC. At least according to its own membership statistics, it constituted the largest single Church in the entire organization. Secondly, because its entry into the ecumenical movement was a major breakthrough in the movement's extension to Orthodoxy, an aspiration long cherished by the WCC's Protestant membership, the opinions of the Russian representatives were received with great seriousness in the deliberations of the WCC. Finally, because the entry of the Russian Church was the epitome of Christian unity transcending political barriers, its participation benefited from the strong theme of ecumenical endeavour to pursue Christian unity regardless of the political hostilities of the moment.

The Russian Orthodox Church was not quick to capitalize on such positional advantages within the WCC. Indeed, the first few years of its participation in the ecumenical movement were marked by a considerable degree of prudence and caution. Russian delegates appeared to be chiefly concerned with consolidating their position within the WCC, gaining many friends and much respect by their careful, considerate conduct. It was only in the latter half of the decade that Russian participants began to advocate their positions more vigorously. In a press conference during the WCC's ' Church and Society ' conference in 1966, Nikodim said, ' When I speak of the needs and problems of the contemporary world, there rises before me the image of the valiant struggling and suffering people of Vietnam and the heart of man cannot but be filled with sacred indignation before the cruel and unlawful actions of the United States in Vietnam.' [5] This more outspoken approach was reiterated two years later at a session of a working group dealing with the problems raised by the 1966 conference :

We see that in the past decade a new world of social relationships has developed—a world has been founded in which the Christian, with all the religious experience of faith and life he possesses, not only can but should find his place. I have in view the socialist countries and the Christians living in them. The new conditions of life do not deprive the Christian of his place in society, but advance the creative transformation of established traditions in conformity with faithfulness to the bases of the Christian faith . . .

The revolutionary process, which is observable at the present time in the entire world and which is acquiring a trend towards even greater spread, demands of the Christian an attentive relationship and a theological evaluation of it, and on this basis demands open acceptance of it and participation in it. If the processes now taking place on earth are attentively observed, it can be seen that the world is being transformed by the revolutionary path, and Christians are called to participate in this revolutionary transformation of the world . . .

The Christian Churches, in the light of contemporary events, are called to intensify their prophetic and didactic service. The task of the Churches is to stir the conscience of the people always and everywhere, so that their conscience may become attentive to the demands of justice and peace in our entire world. This is where concern for the development of humankind and for social justice on earth lead, here the participation of Christians in the struggle for preservation of peace on earth has primary significance, the greatest transgression against which is the aggression of the USA in Vietnam, spawning its cruelty and inhumanity, and truly called a bleeding wound on the body of humanity.[6]

At the Central Committee meeting in Crete in 1967, Nikodim continued to press his position, demanding to know, for example, why the Commission of the Churches on International Affairs (CCIA) had not turned its attention to the problem of racism in the US.[7] In many other instances, it became obvious that the initial years of prudent, almost invisible participation of the Russians in the WCC had given way to a more vigorous and forceful attempt to influence its actions in the latter half of the sixties.

Ultimately, of course, the participation of the Russian Orthodox Church in the WCC reduces to the basic level of the interpersonal relationships established with the various participants engaged in WCC activities. This is particularly true in an organization which has no legislative or governmental functions, but is designed primarily as a forum in which various competing viewpoints and opinions can be brought into vigorous, dynamic, and effective dialogue.

Because of the size and complexity of the WCC, it is difficult to derive any complete, detailed analysis of the people who play important roles in its operations. Generally the WCC has attracted the most sophisticated of Western clergy and laymen, whose breadth of experience provides a difficult challenge for a Church which, like Russian Orthodoxy, has been almost completely isolated from outside influences until quite recently. Relatively liberal political persuasions and progressive social outlooks are heavily represented among the major participants of the WCC, many of whom represent the highest achievement of the heavily emphasized, vastly developed system of Western theological education. Many of the officers, leaders, and participants of the WCC are extraordinarily adept at the intricacies of Church politics, although their primary interest and deep immersion in ecclesiastical affairs may result in rather less understanding of, and experience in, the intricate complexities of secular politics, particularly the subtle and convoluted power politics of international life.

The chief representative of the Russian Orthodox in the WCC, as well as in all other areas of international Church life, is Metropolitan Nikodim. Born Boris Grigorevich Rotov in 1929, he abandoned his studies in a pedagogical institute at the age of eighteen and became a monk, choosing the monastic name Nikodim. Despite his lack of theological education, he was ordained to the priesthood in 1949, and then completed the normal twelve-year theological correspondence course in five years, concurrently serving as parish priest, then rural dean, and finally secretary to his archbishop. After receiving his degree of Candidate of Theology from the Leningrad Academy in 1955, he was sent to Jerusalem in 1957 where he soon became head of the Russian Orthodox mission. On his return to Moscow he became Nikolai's assistant in June 1959 and one year later replaced him as head of the Department of Foreign Affairs of the Moscow Patriarchate, with the rank of bishop.

In 1963, at the age of 34, he was elevated to be Metropolitan of Leningrad and Lagoda, and was without question the most powerful prelate in the Church, second only to the Patriarch.

Nikodim is a man of great ability, immense intelligence, and an impressive array of talents. He can converse in several languages, is able to conduct subtle, complicated, and convincing discussions on a broad range of theological subjects, and has a profound appreciation of the intricacies of international affairs. He is able to respond to almost any line of questioning, including inquiries on potentially embarrassing subjects, with every appearance of spontaneity and sincerity. In his work in the international Christian world, he has been able to build up a broad, all but universal, base of acceptance and confidence among his colleagues from abroad.

The permanent representative of the Moscow Patriarchate at the World Council of Churches was Archpriest Vitaly Borovoy until, in 1967, he joined the staff of the Faith and Order Department, thus becoming the only Russian national employed by the WCC until his transfer early in 1970. Borovoy was profoundly respected in the WCC, with a reputation for complete honesty and candour. His quiet, intelligent ability was of immeasurable benefit in solidifying Russian relations within the WCC, for he spoke frankly, without giving offence, and with no noticeable desire for publicity or public recognition of his services.

In addition, the Moscow Patriarchate enjoys the services of a great number of others, some of them impressively capable, in its interaction with the WCC. This corps of experts within the Church, devoting all or part of their time to international affairs, provides a considerable range of talents and capabilities which can be employed as necessary. The Patriarchate has not enjoyed uniform, unbroken success in providing personnel for its international affairs, however, for certain of its appointees, such as its bishop in Munich, enjoy somewhat less than universal respect. In 1968 Church and State alike suffered the mild embarrassment of having the Secretary of the Patriarchate's permanent representative in Geneva, Archpriest Vladimir Ignaste, defect, receiving political asylum from the Swiss government.[8] Perhaps as a result, the Moscow Patriarchate reduced its manpower in Geneva by recalling its representative, and thereafter had no permanent representation in Geneva other than Borovoy.[9] Such relatively minor annoyances aside, however, the Moscow Patriarchate has been able to provide eminently qualified personnel for the conduct of its foreign affairs.

From the point of view of Soviet foreign policy, the participation of the Russian Church in the WCC has great potential for yielding rich benefits. The Soviet State can expect such participation to accomplish a number of related functions, all of relevance to the desire to strengthen the influence of the USSR in the modern world.

Perhaps the most elementary of the designs of the Soviet State in allowing the Russian Church to join the WCC is simply to ensure that it will maintain some form of a presence in that body. Like nature, a dynamic foreign policy abhors a vacuum, and the mere fact that the Russian Churches are represented may ensure that at the very least the major decisions taken by the WCC will reflect an awareness of their attitudes. Even if no direct influence is to be exerted, provided the WCC takes seriously its commitment to attempt a faithful representation of the desires of its constituents, the Russian presence may induce the WCC to take decisions which, if not positively desired by the Russians, at least will not represent an extreme contradiction of their interests.

An illustration of this effect may possibly be discerned in the difficult process of choosing a successor when the General Secretary (and, indeed, charismatic inspiration) of the WCC, W. A. Visser t'Hooft, reached the mandatory retirement age. The WCC experienced considerable trauma in selecting an acceptable candidate, for in many respects the retiring General Secretary was quite irreplaceable. The final choice, Eugene Carson Blake, who was installed at the beginning of 1967, represented the result of a long and serious search by the leadership of the WCC, and in the manifold considerations which went into the selection process a genuine desire to find a candidate who would be as universally acceptable to the membership as possible seemed to be a major factor.

Blake was one of the most prominent leaders in the US Churches, and prior to his resignation in order to accept the World Council appointment, he had been Stated Clerk (chief executive officer) of the large and influential Presbyterian denomination. Known for a dynamic and progressive attitude in the Church, he had achieved great prominence, along with the Episcopal Bishop James Pike, for initiating a proposal for Church unification which was, at least in American Protestantism, revolutionary. He had long played an active role in national and international Church life, and hence seemed to have excellent qualifications for the task in the WCC.

So far as the Russians are concerned, it would appear that Blake was an eminently acceptable candidate. He was well known to the Russian Orthodox Church, having led the initial US delegation to Russia in

1956, and having made several visits to the country since that time. The official reaction of the Moscow Patriarchate was warmly enthusiastic over his selection, expressing complete satisfaction with the choice.[10] Even if the new chief of staff of the WCC was by no means likely to defer to every desire of the Russian Church or the Soviet State—Blake has demonstrated great independence throughout his career in the Church—the Russian Church could feel that its presence in the WCC had at least received that minimum deference in the matter to assure them that the new candidate would not be unacceptable to them. And indeed, Blake has taken great care to ensure that, despite his American origin, his conduct as General Secretary will not be motivated by any residuum of the political hostilities of the American confrontation with the USSR.

A second benefit which the practitioners of Soviet foreign policy can hope to receive from Russian participation in the WCC is the acquisition of advance information concerning its activities. To be sure, a great many of the WCC's actions are sublimely uninteresting to the secular concerns of Soviet international politics; nevertheless, successful conduct of modern foreign policy depends on accurate knowledge, and the complexities of contemporary international affairs ensure that no significant knowledge, however far removed from the immediate concerns of the country in question, will be without some usefulness in the implementation of foreign policy. Because the WCC reflects attitudes prevalent in a significant portion of the Western public, advance knowledge can facilitate the attempt to form an accurate estimate of the trends of public opinion in the West. And because the WCC retains great power to influence public opinion, information which may be gathered concerning impending decisions and policies can be of some interest to the Soviet State.

Particularly in the early years of Russian participation in the WCC, one of the major goals of the State was that mentioned above: the need to forestall adverse reaction abroad to religious policies which were being applied internally in the USSR. In this regard, the delegates of the USSR were able to render a highly successful service to the State, for, partly because of their efforts, it was several years before knowledge of actual conditions in the Russian Churches began to penetrate into the WCC. Russian churchmen were careful to state that their Churches enjoyed excellent conditions in the USSR, and at no time offered any public criticism or equivocation which might detract from the State's desired image of complete religious toleration.

In its initial entry into the WCC, the Russian Orthodox Church demonstrated its willingness to serve in this regard. The official application for membership stated that 22,000 churches were functioning in the Moscow Patriarchate.[11] If this estimate was somewhat less unrealistic than the most extreme claims of the previous decade, which occasionally went as high as 30,000, it was still far from accurate. According to secular sources in the USSR, at no time since World War II has the number of Orthodox churches exceeded 16,000, and, in addition, the rising antireligious campaign had begun to take a considerable toll by the end of 1961, when the Russians were received into membership in the WCC. In 1962 a Soviet source stated that only 11,500 churches were still functioning, and this figure was privately confirmed by Russian churchmen.[12] By the end of Khrushchev's reign the number had declined to approximately 7,500 remaining churches.[13] Nevertheless, the figure offered by the Moscow Patriarchate in its application for membership was not publicly challenged in the WCC and, indeed, remains acceptable to a large portion of the WCC membership. Especially during the first part of the decade, any difficulties which the Church was experiencing at home were not reflected in the participation of the Russian Church in the WCC, and certainly the danger that movements protesting against Soviet treatment of religious citizens might arise within the WCC was successfully averted.

Similarly, no great embarrassment has been occasioned to the Soviet State by the public attitudes of the WCC concerning the *Initsiativniki* controversy in the Russian Baptist Church (which is also a member of the WCC). In November 1967 the General Secretary of the WCC made a statement concerning a document which had been received from the USSR appealing for aid, and giving specific information on over 200 Baptists currently in prison:

The World Council of Churches is studying the document closely. Because of its concern for both religious liberty and unity within its member churches, it is seeking direct contact with the competent authorities in the USSR particularly with leaders of the Baptist Church, who have been asked to comment on the document and evaluate it.[14]

Any further action in the case was not made public, and in the report concerning the actions taken by the Executive Committee in its meeting at the end of January 1968 there was no further mention of this affair, although the meeting did endorse protests on behalf of political prisoners in Greece and South Africa.[15]

Of the several examples of specific successes achieved in the attempt to shield domestic religious policies from foreign view, the most useful to the State occurred in 1966. On 18 March, in response to the growing challenge of the *Initsiativniki*, amendments to the Penal Code were promulgated in the USSR, which specified a great number of criminal offences in the religious field, and also revised the prescribed penalties. These new laws occasioned considerable apprehension in the West, and on 26 May the WCC's *Ecumenical Press Service* published an analysis of these laws, emphasizing the reduction of certain sentences without discerning the increase in severity which was also contained. On 31 August V. Kuroyedov, the chief spokesman for the State's religious policy, found it expedient to utilize this analysis in the course of a stern attack in *Izvestiia* against the *Initsiativniki*, in which he gave an official explanation of the new legislation :

Essentially it is a question of the easing of punishment in relation to first offenders against the law on separation of church and state. However, increased penalties are established for those citizens who have already been sentenced for such offenses and similarly if they have expanded any activities planned to secure such contravention.

Such an influential church publication as the *Bulletin of the World Council of Churches* (No. 17, 26 May 1966) wrote :

' At the beginning of April various press agencies published communications from Moscow, according to which restrictions on religious freedom had been introduced by a decree of the Supreme Soviet in Russia (RSFSR). A study of the text, which in fact contains three decrees, demonstrated that these decrees basically confirm, define and in some instances introduce greater flexibility into the laws which already exist. In contradiction to what was published in the newspapers, not one of these decrees prohibits free collections designed to meet the needs of churches, nor is it recognized that discrimination against people in connection with their religious adherence can be legal.

' In order to illustrate the easing of conditions which previously existed, it may be noted that some violations of the law which were previously punished by imprisonment now merely carry a fine of up to 50 rubles . . .' [16]

In actual fact, this article in *Izvestiia* initiated a new wave of arrest and incarceration of the members and leaders of the *Initsiativniki* movement, and the provisions of the new legislation were liberally applied against the defendants.

It should not be imagined, however, that the aspiration of Soviet foreign policy to prevent foreign realization of the religious situation within the USSR enjoyed complete success in the WCC. At the meeting of the Executive Committee in February 1964 at Odessa, Frederick Nolde, speaking for the CCIA, made a strong recommendation for endorsement of freedom of belief for believers and atheists as well, including the right to ' manifest it in society '.[17] And at a similar meeting in February 1969 the General Secretary referred to the difficult circumstances which face the Churches in atheist countries. ' Our task ', he said, ' is to attempt to keep in touch with all of them.' [18]

The primary objective which Soviet foreign policy hoped to achieve from Russian participation in the WCC was, of course, to influence its activities in such a way that its decisions and actions would be conformable to Soviet interests as much as possible. Considerable benefits might result if the actions of the WCC served to support Soviet endeavours, and to detract from the support of opposing measures. In this regard, several important successes were achieved, although the actions of the WCC were by no means pleasing to the Soviet State in every instance, and even though these results were achieved more often by default than because of the influence of the Russian participants. Some actions of the WCC that were based on other considerations altogether did, indeed, tend to buttress the Soviet position, but it should be noted that in many of these cases the participants of the WCC by and large had no aspiration whatsoever to support one political power or another in these disputes, and, in fact, were quite often indifferent to whether such actions, which the WCC felt were right, could be utilized by partisan, secular interests. Nevertheless, Soviet foreign policy could derive some benefit from certain of the actions of the WCC, and if participation of the Russian Orthodox Church in the WCC was instrumental in securing these benefits, the Soviet State could feel amply justified in its decision to allow the Church to become engaged in the ecumenical movement.

In the East-West confrontation, it quickly became evident that actions of the WCC might be helpful to Soviet endeavours. One of the earliest instances occurred during the Cuban missile crisis in 1962. At the height of the crisis, on 2 October, the WCC's General Secretary, Visser t'Hooft, the Chairman of the Central Committee, Ernest Payne, and Nolde, head of the CCIA, issued the following brief statement:

Taking their stand on statements made by the World Council of Churches' Assemblies, the Committees and Officers of the World Council of Churches have on several occasions expressed their concern and regret when governments have taken unilateral military action against other governments. The Officers of the World Council of Churches consider it, therefore, their duty to express grave concern and regret concerning the action which the USA government has felt it necessary to take with regard to Cuba and fervently hope that every government concerned will exercise the greatest possible restraint in order to avoid a worsening of the international tension.[19]

This statement elicited a mixed reaction. One thousand delegates at a conference of the Lutheran Church in America then in session voted overwhelmingly to repudiate it, on grounds that it ' speaks out against the government of the United States in the Cuban Crisis.' [20] Nikodim, however, in a communication to Visser t'Hooft, stated:

We approve your condemnation in the name of the World Council of Churches of these dangerous acts of the American government against the Republic of Cuba, of which we learned from the report of the *Agence France Presse*, and express confidence that the World Council of Churches also henceforth will not diminish its strength in this direction, until by the mercy of God the dangerous conflict will receive a favorable resolution.[21]

With regard to Vietnam, although the WCC made an important contribution to the massive revulsion against the war which eventually helped to frustrate the original designs of the US government, the Russian participants were hardly satisfied with the WCC's endeavours in this issue. The WCC was careful to avoid extreme statements against the war such as, for example, were current in the CPC, and while by no means softening its condemnation of US actions, it also tried to achieve a measure of balance by recognizing that other parties to the conflict bore a portion of the responsibility. In particular, the WCC gave great support to the efforts of the United Nations to resolve the conflict, and almost without exception, it refrained from giving unconditional support to the point of view advocated by the USSR.[22] A crisis of sorts occurred in August 1967 when Russian members of the Central Committee meeting in Crete prevented unanimous acceptance of the resolution on Vietnam by voting against it.

From our point of view, the origin of the Vietnam tragedy is the entirely unjustified military intervention of the USA in the internal life of the Vietnamese people. The withdrawal of the American troops from the territory, without any condition, is absolutely necessary, and the Vietnam problem must be settled on the basis of the Geneva Agreements.

We ask for this special opinion to be included in the minutes of the meetings of the Central Committee of the World Council of Churches.[23]

In this case, even though its specific recommendations were not met, the Russian delegation was able to ensure that its position would receive attention, thereby salvaging some small additional benefit for the interests of Soviet foreign policy.

Similarly, WCC grants allocated for aid to American military deserters and for strengthening social services in Poland were not altogether irrelevant to the interests of Soviet foreign policy. The former, by making a contribution, however small, to the reduction of morale in the US armed services, could be interpreted by practitioners of Soviet foreign policy as consonant with their desire to reduce the military effectiveness of the USSR's major competitor. The latter, announced by the WCC's *Ecumenical Press Service* on 19 November 1970, consisted of an agreement signed with the Polish government whereby the WCC was to make a direct donation of $252,000 for medical and social services. Not only might this serve as an implicit endorsement of the Polish government's social policies, it also provided a curious commentary on Church-State relations in Poland: although the project was ' to be implemented by the Polish Ecumenical Council ', the agreement itself was presented as a bilateral contract between the WCC and the Polish government's Ministry of Health and Social Welfare. There was no mention of Poland's dominant religious charitable organization, the Catholic Caritas Society, in the communiqué.

With regard to the Third World, it would seem that significant, albeit not unalloyed, success was achieved. The exceedingly vigorous opposition of the WCC to racial discrimination in South Africa and Rhodesia was not entirely dissimilar to the position of the USSR (and that of a great many other countries) on the matter, although it hardly seems likely, in view of the ecumenical movement's great concern for racial justice, that the attitudes of the Russian members were of any particular influence in this matter. In the Nigerian Civil War, although the WCC refrained from supporting the predominantly Christian Biafrans in the dispute, it also refrained from taking the Nigerian side, as the USSR was doing, but instead endeavoured to give aid to the suffering of both sides.[24]

Much greater success was achieved with regard to the general attitude of the WCC towards the Third World, for the WCC's trend towards radical solutions to the problems of the underdeveloped world was, in many respects, directly applicable to the approaches advocated in Soviet foreign policy. With its highly developed concern for social justice and the alleviation of suffering, the WCC devoted great attention to the needs and problems of the Third World, both concretely with regard to the specific concerns of its member Churches from the under-developed nations, and in the search for solutions to the general problem of the great imbalance prevalent in the modern world. As has been noted, the Russian Churches consistently advocated radical solutions to the problem. At the WCC's Church and Society conference in 1966, there semed to be a developing consensus in favour of drastic measures, with other points of view which suggested more gradual, peaceful processes of change receiving rather less attention. When the WCC's General Assembly at Uppsala in 1968 advocated Christian support of revolution, not excluding violence in certain circumstances, the WCC's position with regard to the problems of the Third World had moved significantly closer to the approach long since taken in the Soviet doctrines regarding the colonial and neo-colonial countries, and the USSR could hope to benefit from the WCC's position in pursuing its own foreign policy endeavours in the Third World.

Matters progressed rapidly thereafter.[25] In 1969 the Central Committee of the WCC established a Programme to Combat Racism, with a Special Fund of $200,000 (and appeals were issued for an additional $300,000 in contributions) for aid to organizations of the racially oppressed. By 1969 the Fund had grown to $285,000, of which the Executive Committee decided in September 1970 to allocate $200,000 to nineteen anti-racist organizations, fourteen of them in southern Africa. Grants of from $2,000 to $20,000 were made to these organizations ' irrespective of whether they use military means to achieve freedom '. Immediately a storm of controversy arose, erupting into one of the hottest debates in the history of the WCC. According to the WCC's *Ecumenical Press Service,*

Almost the whole white press has fallen for a few subtle changes in vocabulary. Support for victims of racism became support for murder and terrorism. Liberation movements were called guerilla movements or terrorist movements, words so emotion-loaded that they make a factual discussion much more difficult.

Spokesmen for the WCC defended the decision vigorously. It was pointed out that the action was in harmony with the WCC tradition of giving aid to people in need, as had been done for ' Arab refugees, Russian refugees, American deserters, war victims in North and South Vietnam, Lagos and Biafra '. It was emphasized that the funds were to go to ' organizations whose major purpose is in harmony with the ecumenical consensus against racism', and that 'the 20-year-old consensus against discrimination is finally being activated'. It was noted that 'the grants were made with the understanding that the money would not be used for military purposes', but for welfare, scholarships, medical needs, information programmes, and the like. However, the WCC was quite candid that it had sought to retain no control over the actual utilization of the grants:

The new factor in the struggle against racism is the request of the victims themselves to be recognised as partners and not just recipients of charity. The blacks want solidarity, not charity. They want a share of power to be able to negotiate. The quest for shared power is the quest for identity and dignity.

This request for a transfer of power was at the heart of the discussion which led to the Special Fund. For that reason the grants were made without control. From several sides this has been criticized. Some wanted to send only medicaments and similar items to Africa; others would like to establish donor-controlled centres in Africa (as was done during the Nigeria crisis) in order to make sure the money was not misused. A third group pleaded that help go only to the churches.

The trouble with these suggestions, the intent of which cannot be doubted, is that they are regarded as out of date by the victims of racism. It would mean a return to the period in which the donor could (would) not trust his partner on the other side.

At the time of writing, the controversy continues unabated, and there is no means of predicting its outcome, or what effects the WCC will experience, beneficial or otherwise, from the stimulation of this debate and the intense interest which it has generated.

From the point of view of Soviet foreign policy, however, the immediate consequences of this decision can only be appraised positively, and the WCC decision represents an important—and possibly quite unexpected—windfall. On 25 June 1970 *Izvestiia* devoted an article to the revolutionary movements in southern Africa, taking considerable pride in the fact that the USSR energetically supports them. Three revolutionary organizations were singled out for special mention, FRELIMO, the MPLA, and the PAIGC (operating in Mozambique, Angola, and Portuguese Guinea, respectively), all of which were, according to *Izvestiia*, receiving arms from the Soviet Union. All three of these organizations were listed among the recipients of WCC grants in September. The addition of funds from the WCC thus promised to be of direct benefit to Soviet foreign policy in these three instances. In view of the fact that the aid was given without controls, Soviet practitioners could contemplate the possibility of these donations being assigned to a general fund, thereby reducing the needs which the USSR had been meeting, or, if reductions in Soviet aid were not contemplated, augmenting the capabilities of these groups which the USSR had decided it was in her own interest to support. Even should the funds be used for non-military purposes, the Biafran experience demonstrated that armed insurrection involves the total resources of the dissidents; the lack of food and medicines contributed no less to the defeat of the Biafran insurgents than did the shortage of arms. In any event, the USSR could contemplate an increased yield from its aid to these organizations however the WCC funds were utilized; from the point of view of cost-effectiveness the Soviet investment could expect to benefit from any additional donations to these groups, whatever the source of the gifts.

During the first part of the decade WCC attitudes with regard to Greece and Turkey were not entirely compatible with the desires of the Russian members. In the Cyprus dispute the WCC supported the Anglo-American plan; [26] in 1964 it cabled the Turkish government urging that the rights of the Ecumenical Patriarchate in Turkey be protected.[27] After the *coup d'état* in Greece, however, the actions of the military government provided an issue on which the WCC found itself largely in agreement with the Russian Church. The Executive Committee in February 1968 authorized the General Secretary to visit Greece in order to attempt to intercede with the authorities in matters of social justice and freedom, and the CCIA, which had already lodged one protest with the Greek Prime Minister concerning political prisoners, promised to issue another and to conduct two investigations of the matter.[28] These actions were bitterly opposed by the Greek Church, and it announced that it was withdrawing its delegation from the forthcoming General Assembly on grounds of the WCC's interference in the internal affairs of Greece.[29]

Although the influence of the Russian delegation almost certainly was not the primary factor in the decision, the position taken by the WCC with regard to events in the Middle East was eminently satisfactory from the point of view of Soviet foreign policy. The WCC refrained from succumbing to that powerful wave of support for Israel in the Six-Day War which swept through the West in the Churches as well as among the general public. On 7 June 1967 WCC leaders gave their support to the efforts of the UN Security Council to effect a cease-fire,[30] and on 22 June the WCC position was officially stated: 'We do not believe that the Israeli-Arab conflict is a political issue on which moral duty clearly requires us to take an absolute stand for or against either side.'[31] The WCC sent aid to the refugees of both sides, although in the circumstances such non-partisan relief services were of more significance for the Arabs than the Israelis (there were not many Israeli refugees after the brief war), and on 17 August the United Arab Republic expressed its thanks to the WCC for the aid to refugees.[32] The Central Committee of the WCC on 31 August resolved that a solution should be sought based on Israeli withdrawal to its previous boundaries, international guarantees of the territorial integrity of all nations in the Middle East, permission for all refugees to return, and free access to the holy places for all faiths.[33]

It seems likely that the major factor influencing the WCC position was consideration of the desires, positions, and situation of the WCC member Churches in the Middle East. In July, for example, Bishop Samuel of the Coptic Church in Egypt had urged the WCC to call a special meeting on the Middle East Crisis.[34] Indeed, in view of the passions of the Arab populations, any ill-considered action by the WCC would almost certainly have resulted in immensely adverse effects on its member Churches in the Arab countries. (The same considerations may be reflected in the actions taken by the Vatican, which also resisted the tide of support for Israel in the crisis.)

Nevertheless, the position taken by the WCC was quite compatible with the approach Soviet foreign policy was advocating in the Middle East, despite the fact that the Russian delegation refused to support the Central Committee resolution of 31 August:

The points that ' no decisions should be made via armed force ', and that ' no country should retain or annex the territory of another state ' are suspended in the air in the background of the general, nebulous context of the document. The points on international guarantees of security, on the reduction of armaments and the like are inadequately based, for in the document all this is not demanded as the first and decisive step toward the resolution of the problem of liberating the occupied territories and cessation of military demonstrations on the part of the state which began the war with the sole purpose of extending its own territory at the cost of neighboring sovereign states ... Peace and brotherhood of the peoples, collaboration for the development of all areas of the Near East—this is what must prevail. But all this is [only] possible with the complete exclusion of the imperialistic context, which has conditioned the eruption and continuation right up to the present time of tension in the Near East.[35]

Despite these criticisms from the Russian members, which, however energetically they were pressed, were quite insubstantial, the position taken by the WCC was fully applicable to the general position taken by Soviet Middle Eastern policy.

The Soviet State achieved rather disappointing results in its attempts to influence WCC attitudes towards its international activities conducted in Eastern Europe. Despite the wishes of the Russian members, the WCC refused to give unqualified endorsement to the CPC and, ultimately, reacted with outright condemnation to the Soviet policy of subjugation, by force if necessary, of its dominions in Eastern Europe. However, at the time of the invasion of Prague an immediate success was achieved in the WCC which, from the point of view of Soviet foreign policy, was most welcome and beneficial.

The sudden invasion of Prague on 21 August 1968 was a profound shock, particularly for that large portion of the Western public which had hoped and believed that Stalinism had given way to a transformed, more humanitarian attitude in the USSR. Massive protest arose immediately, with outspoken condemnation of the invasion arising from nearly every sector of society in the West, including Western Communist parties. The Pope, the Archbishop of Canterbury, the US National Council of Churches, and, indeed, an immense number of Church organizations issued strong reactions and protests almost immediately upon verification of the news from Czechoslovakia.

The immediate reaction of the WCC, however, was less impassioned. On 22 August the General Secretary sent the following cable to the WCC member Churches of Czechoslovakia and of the five invading powers:

Please advise promptly attitude or position of your church on recent events in Czechoslovakia. CCIA sending to its commissioners and national commissions quotations from past statements issued by churches together relevant to present situation. Until things become clearer I am not proposing any new statement.[36]

The moderation and restraint of this reaction to the invasion was quite surprising in the context of the times, and contrasted markedly with the unequivocal reaction taken by the WCC in response to the similar invasion of Hungary twelve years earlier. Although the action did protect the WCC from making an ill-considered reaction in the crisis of the moment, giving it time to make a considered evaluation of a situation which may have seemed uncertain, its consequences and implications were not altogether felicitous for all parties concerned.

While this response to the invasion might seem a justifiable attempt to abide by the obligation of the officers of the WCC to represent the interests of the members, rather than expressing their own personal attitudes, it was not, in fact, altogether in the interests of these Churches to seek their reactions. The invasion placed the Churches of Eastern Europe and the USSR in an exceedingly tense situation, and the dilemma caused by having to take a public stand was acute. To justify the invasion was difficult from the standpoint of Communist doctrine, and almost impossible from a position of Christian ethics. It would be most difficult for a Church to support the action, even with the aid of the most intricate of rationalizations. In view of the tensions of the times, the risk that severity applied against Czechoslovak non-conformity might also spread over into society as a whole was acute, and the best counsel for the Churches would have been to remain quiet, attracting as little attention to themselves as possible until the crisis had passed. However, the telegram from the WCC placed the issue squarely in front of them, and the Churches of Czechoslovakia and the five invading countries were forced to take a stand.

In actual fact, this request for advice was quite unnecessary, for there could be no question of what the public attitudes of the Churches would be. In a controlled society the Church enjoys only a narrow latitude, and to denounce its government's actions, particularly in a time of crisis, is to court massive retaliation. The public reactions to the invasion actually taken by these Churches proved to be to support the action of their governments without reservation, or to remain silent altogether.

From the point of view of Soviet foreign policy, however, the WCC's refusal to add its immense weight to the chorus of immediate denunciation was an important windfall. For the USSR to invade one of its most Westernized subject States, situated on Western Europe's border, entailed a risk, however slight, of reprisal from the West, with the consequent possibility of a major war erupting. The delay of even a very few days in mounting such a reaction would reduce its likelihood by several orders of magnitude. Hence the level of protest in the West was of some importance in the operation's success, and for an influential force in Western public opinion, such as the WCC, to refrain from protesting, or even to delay its reaction, was of immediate benefit to Soviet interests in the Czech crisis.

After the immediate crisis had passed, however, the World Council of Churches did issue a statement on 28 August concerning the invasion, and by no means was it such as would please the Soviet State :

We deplore the military intervention into the internal affairs of Czechoslovakia, a small, allied, friendly, neighboring state, by the governments
of the USSR, Poland, East Germany, Hungary and Bulgaria.

.   .   .   .

We fear the effect of this ill-considered action by the USSR and its allies,
because of its damage to the confidence of peace-loving people everywhere,
a confidence upon which alone world peace can be established.

We appeal to the government of the USSR to reconsider the policy
which dictated the military intervention, to remove all its troops from
Czechoslovakia at the earliest possible moment, and to renounce the use
of force or its threat upon its allies . . .[37]

The Russian Orthodox Church objected vigorously to this statement.
On 14 September Patriarch Aleksii protested against it in an open letter
to the President of the Central Committee :

We raise the question : do you and your colleagues have sufficient basis to
make such categorical assertions? The answer, in our opinion, should be
negative. For it is known to all that Czechoslovakia is a component part
of the socialist commonwealth, that Czechoslovakia and the Soviet Union,
Czechoslovakia and Bulgaria, Hungary, the DDR and Poland are allied
with each other by bilateral agreements on friendship, mutual aid and
co-operation both in ideological and in practical questions and that they
are all members of the Warsaw Treaty organization, among whose tasks,
as the texts of the treaty agreements state, is the mutual defense of the
socialism and independence of these states . . .

.   .   .   .

Furthermore, nothing is said in your document concerning the reason
for the temporary entry of the troops of the five countries allied with the
CSR into the territory of Czechoslovakia (they have made clear and
specific statements on this), which was the necessity of defense of the
socialist order in Czechoslovakia, to which the people of this country are
devoted and which was under threat from the destructive activity of
anti-socialist powers.

Therefore we are convinced that what took place on 21 August of this
year averted serious bloodshed and, possibly, international armed
conflict.[38]

Thus the participation of the Russian Church had not been successful
in preventing hostile reactions in the WCC to the actions of the Soviet
government. However, the fact that the expression of such reactions
was delayed by one week, at the end of which the crisis had receded

and Western intervention was not even a remote possibility, was highly beneficial to the successful achievement of the goals of Soviet policy in the Czech crisis.

In summary, the participation of the Russian Churches in the World Council of Churches has resulted in concrete successes as well as in a number of failures from the point of view of Soviet foreign policy. However, it would be unrealistic of the USSR, and certainly uncharacteristic of its pragmatic approach to foreign policy, to expect absolute success in any endeavour in the complex international world. Any successes at all are to be welcomed, and, particularly in view of the magnitude of the overall benefits which have accrued to the Soviet State since the entry of the Russian Churches into the World Council of Churches, the activities of the Russian Churches in the ecumenical movement must be assessed as highly beneficial from the viewpoint of Soviet foreign policy.

10   Trends and Prospects

AT the beginning of the 1970s the role of religion in Soviet foreign policy appeared to be in a transitional phase. The patterns of activities of the Russian Churches in international affairs had undergone an evolution during the previous decade, and towards its close modifications were becoming more and more apparent. Certain types of activity which had been prominent during the sixties were being discarded, some of the approaches which had yielded much success were approaching an impasse, while other experiments were appearing, and, indeed, the geographic interests of the Russian Church appeared to be shifting. In the seventies new kinds of co-operation between the international affairs of the Churches and the interests of the State would have to develop if the established dimension of religion in Soviet foreign policy were to be continued.

In particular, the innovations introduced by Khrushchev were being augmented or modified. More than ever, the USSR had established itself as a global power by the close of the decade, and if religion were to continue to perform a function in Soviet foreign policy, its activities would have to remain on a world-wide basis. The limited-achievement approach was rapidly falling from favour, and in its place a more insistent attitude was appearing. Although public opinion continued to receive a measure of respect in the total execution of foreign policy, it was by no means considered crucial, and in particular, the heavy emphasis on creating a favourable public image for the USSR, in which the Churches had excelled, was being displaced by a greater emphasis on achieving results directly useful to the concrete interests of Soviet foreign policy.

There was a pronounced trend towards a more vigorous, uncompromising, adamant approach in the activities of the Russian Church as the decade drew to a close. As has been indicated, during Khrushchev's reign the foreign activities of the Church had been characterized by a cautious, largely unobtrusive pattern of activity designed to achieve a solid, well-founded position for the Church in the international sphere of activities. By 1966, when Khrushchev had been replaced and the collective leadership was gaining confidence and stability in its command of the USSR, this former approach gave way to a more vigorous,

140

assertive pattern as the Church, apparently satisfied that a secure foundation had been laid, attempted to achieve the desired results more directly than it had done in the earlier part of the decade. Particularly in its activities in the World Council of Churches, the Russian delegation began to adhere to a harder line, much more outspoken in its positions and with much less tolerance for disagreement or for modification of its desired goals.

In particular, the tactics of the Church began increasingly to depart from the limited-achievement approach characteristic of the Khrushchev period, and to return towards the totalistic approach of the Stalin period. Less leeway was allowed for acceptance of subsidiary, largely irrelevant issues in order to facilitate achievement of the major goal, and there was much less patience with partial, rather than complete, successes. Whereas the earlier pattern had been marked by a willingness to accept small results in the hope of eventually developing them to the desired dimensions, by the close of the decade there was more forceful insistence on complete acceptance of the interpretation, resolution, or policy advocated by the Russian Church. The denunciation of the largely favourable resolution of the WCC with regard to the Israeli-Arab conflict in 1967 may provide an example of this trend towards less tolerance of incomplete results, and the history of the Christian Peace Conference after the invasion of Prague displayed an almost complete abandonment of the tolerant, limited-achievement approach which had brought so much success to the CPC, and a resumption of a hard line of insistence on total, or near total, conformity to the desires transmitted from above.

This new approach required a much greater degree of boldness on the part of the Russian churchmen than had characterized their activities in the first part of the decade. When their chief assignment had been to create a favourable impression and build solid relations, outspokenness was somewhat of a rarity among them. Now, however, the time for building had obviously been declared over, and a more dynamic, assertive approach was indicated, a readiness to press for maximum achievements whenever possible.

Naturally, this new approach necessitated that risks be taken. An aggressive approach must involve a degree of risk. Particularly in dealing with the subtleties of religion, boldness carries great danger of alienation of one's colleagues in other societies and other religions. Apparently it was decided that the foundation which had been built was sufficiently solid to tolerate such aggressiveness, as in the case of the

WCC, where the increased outspokenness of the Russian participants was nicely calculated—or fortuitous—and did not result in any noticeable alienation. Or else, as in the case of the CPC, it was decided that unless the participants were willing to adhere to the desired programme, any minor successes which might be achieved were not worth bothering with, and as a result so much severity was introduced after the invasion of Czechoslovakia that almost total alienation ensued among the movement's adherents.

Generally, the Churches appeared to enjoy a great deal less latitude in the new policy which had begun to crystallize at the close of the decade. Their activities displayed much less flexibility than before, and their interests were able to extend over a much smaller range. In their conduct of international affairs, the Churches seemed persuaded to adhere much more closely to the programme of Soviet policy, and to operate on a much more restricted basis, with less freedom of attitudes, conduct, and interests than they had enjoyed earlier in the decade.

The general trend, then, was away from the Khrushchevian pattern of subtlety and latitude, and back towards the more restricted approaches of the Stalin era. By no means did it seem that the pattern of international Church activity which had prevailed during the early cold war had been reintroduced completely, or that the international affairs of the Church had been restricted again within the excessively narrow limits which had prevailed then. But it was plain that the approaches introduced during the reign of Khrushchev were no longer to be employed, and the trend was towards Stalin's pattern, rather than in the other direction.

In this regard, the international activity of the Church was following the general trend of Soviet society in many aspects of domestic life. The increasing imposition of controls within society, and the State's vigorous intolerance of dissent, both among the intelligentsia and in the religious population, seemed to indicate that the tendency to allow a measure of latitude within the society was being replaced by a partial—but by no means a total—return to the Stalinist pattern of strict control. In view of the severity with which this pattern of greater control was being applied in Eastern Europe, it is not at all unnatural that the international activities of the Churches should display somewhat less latitude than earlier in the decade.

The implication is that the activities of the Russian Churches can expect considerably less success than earlier in the decade. Certainly the circle of Western and Third World churchmen who can be reached by the new policy will be somewhat smaller than those who could be effectively engaged in activities of a more tolerant nature. If the limited-achievement policy is to give way to a more totalistic insistence, Soviet foreign policy will be able to enjoy none of the partial, but nevertheless useful, successes to which it became accustomed during the sixties. This reduction in the number or breadth of successes achievable, however, might appear to the leadership to represent only a marginal loss, one which, in terms of concrete profitability, was only of questionable value to the interests of Soviet foreign policy. If the attempt to achieve direct, unambiguous results by a more aggressive approach proves successful, the gains might be considered more than sufficient compensation for the losses inherent in the revised approach to Church foreign activities.

At the beginning of the seventies, the geographical balance of Church activities throughout the world was in a state of transition, with some of the old priorities remaining valid, others of them reduced or scheduled to be replaced by new ones.

The participation of the Russian Churches in the World Council of Churches had not been subject to any significant change with the waning of the decade. The position of the Russians was secure, with a solidly entrenched base of operations established in the WCC structure. They formed a major component of the WCC, and even though the tactics employed in WCC functions had changed towards a more vigorous attempt to assert their influence, the Russian Churches retained a stable, effective, and important position in the WCC. There were no signs of possible alienation due to the greater aggressiveness of the Russian delegations, and, indeed, many of the developing trends towards a more radical approach to the world's problems (e.g. in the attitudes to Third World problems) gave some indication that the Russian Church enjoyed favourable conditions for the new approach; outspoken and extreme solutions seemed acceptable to many of the representatives at WCC functions, particularly among the youth.

The WCC itself, however, was faced with the prospect of its own transformation, at least to some degree. The general impatience with traditional moderation, which was receiving increasingly strong representation at WCC meetings, raised the possibility that the organization itself might be impelled towards more radical positions, a process which, if carried beyond a certain limit, would contribute to that endemic threat of polarization within Western Christianity between liberal and conservative sentiments. In the adamantly conservative denominations, the WCC was already considered rather irrevelant to the interest of the local church, and if large proportions of the members of major denominations should become disenchanted, if the WCC should gain any considerable reputation for a predictably radical approach too far in advance of its constituency, its influence in Western Christendom would be significantly curtailed. Naturally, in such a case it would have somewhat less interest for Soviet foreign policy than otherwise.

At the close of the sixties, however, this remained a fairly remote possibility, and the WCC's stature among the Churches remained undiminished and immensely influential. Furthermore, the increasing progress being made in conversations with Roman Catholicism promised to offset any such dangers by a large margin, at least for the immediate future. Hence, from the point of view of Soviet foreign policy, the WCC remained one of the most important areas of the international activity of the Russian Church.

Furthermore, the Russian Churches had become so deeply immersed in the WCC that it would be exceedingly difficult for them to disengage themselves, even should the ecumenical movement suffer some loss of influence in the world. The post-Stalin activity of the Russian Church in international affairs had been built around the twin centres of the WCC and the Christian Peace Conference. With the collapse of the CPC, not only was the Russian Church deprived of a reserve position to which it could repair if participation in the WCC should no longer be considered worthwhile, it retained no central focus for its activities other than the World Council of Churches. Many of the other areas of activity would have to be reorganized entirely, or even begun anew, if it should become necessary to terminate participation in the WCC. Hence there seemed every indication that the Russian Church would continue its WCC activities without substantial reduction well past the end of the sixties.

The East-West conflict remains an area with much potential for Russian Church activities. The gradual increase in liberal or even radical sentiments of the later sixties had not significantly abated by the close of the decade, and there was every indication that the Russian Church would continue to find sympathetic responses to its position of rejection of all wars, especially those attempting to frustrate national liberation movements, of advocating total and unconditional disarmament, of supporting revolution in the face of social or economic injustice, and the like.

Furthermore, the general tendency of the US government to reduce its global commitments in the wake of Vietnam had not yet been tested and, at least until such sentiments were reversed, Soviet foreign policy could expect multiplied opportunities to develop in its perennial confrontation with the West. In such conditions, there would be every likelihood that numerous opportunities would arise for the Church to render expanded and increasingly important services.

The Third World presented the greatest difficulty for the foreign activities of the Russian Church at the beginning of the seventies. The great emphasis which had been placed on the CPC in Third World activities caused many of the activities successfully pursued during the sixties virtually to collapse when the CPC ceased to be an effective instrument of Church foreign affairs. In large measure, the Church faced the task of starting all over again in the Third World, with relatively few programmes from the sixties which continued to be viable. The Third World continued to offer the most immediate opportunities for expansion of Soviet influence in the world, and hence if the Russian Church were to continue to render service to Soviet foreign policy, it would have to devise ways of bringing the Third World once more within its purview. But there were few indications of what forms the activities of the Russian Church in the Third World would take.

Africa was especially problematical. With the collapse of the CPC, the only fruits which remained were those which had been developed independently of the CPC. In view of the vast emphasis which the latter received in the African activities of the Eastern Churches, relatively little remained upon which to build. To devise new methods of acquiring an influence in that troubled continent would be a major undertaking, demanding immense efforts if it were to be successfully accomplished in the seventies.

To some degree, the impotence of the Russian Church in Africa was not a critical problem, for at the start of the seventies Africa seemed to rank rather low on the scale of Soviet foreign policy priorities. The political instability and the insurmountable social and economic problems of the African nations offered little attraction for the USSR, which had more immediate and much more promising prospects elsewhere. But in the struggle for influence in the world the African continent could not be ignored indefinitely, and sooner or later would demand some energy, both from Soviet foreign policy and from the Russian Church.

Immense opportunities were available in the Middle East, however. Soviet success in establishing a sphere of influence was growing rapidly as the seventies began, and the Russian Church and, more particularly,

Soviet Islam, could expect to find a rapidly increasing area of service there. In many respects the revised approach which had come into vogue in the foreign activities of the Russian Church, whereby quiet subtlety had given way to outspoken bluntness, seemed admirably suited to the developing sphere of activities in the Middle East. In the unsubtle atmosphere of the Arab countries, as contrasted with the sophisticated understatement of Europe and America, a degree of stridency prevails, and the progressive outspokenness of the Russian clerics could continue indefinitely without becoming unacceptable to the Arab audience or even, indeed, approaching the level of overstatement which is their staple.

The competition between the Russian Orthodox Church and the Ecumenical Patriarchate was of direct importance in the attempt of the Russian Church to increase its influence in the Middle East. Should Moscow succeed in wresting pre-eminence away from Istanbul, should the Russian Patriarch become the unquestioned leader in Orthodoxy, the services which it could render to a well-entrenched Soviet policy operating in an established sphere of influence would be enormous. In view of the abrupt escalation of the challenge to the Ecumenical Patriarchate engineered by the Russian Orthodox Church late in 1969, it was not possible to foresee the directions which might be taken in Russian Orthodox Middle Eastern affairs should Soviet foreign policy continue to enjoy increasing success in the area.

The Latin American activities of the Russian Church remained practically bankrupt as the seventies began, just as they had been during the preceding decade (excepting the evanescent successes the CPC had been able to achieve). No particularly promising opportunities in South America were in sight. However, the area remains a critical field for the struggle for influence, and Soviet foreign policy was by no means ignoring it. Hence if the Russian Church should be able to develop any important programme of activities in South America, this would be a useful area in which to render service to the Soviet State. Any significant activities there, however, remain largely contingent on the establishment of some sort of harmonious relationship with Roman Catholicism, and the endeavours to effect a *rapprochement* between Russian Orthodoxy and Rome were still some distance from success. However, the important attempt of the Russian Church to decrease the distance from Rome late in 1969 would indicate a continuing, vigorous effort in this direction. Should success be achieved and a far-reaching *rapprochement* with Rome develop, then the Russian Church might begin to examine South America as an area of great opportunity.

In Asia, Soviet Buddhists were becoming more active, and the interests of the Russian Church in Asia appeared to have suffered relatively few adverse effects due to the collapse of the CPC. In India, relations with the Malabar Church had been bilateral and seemed to remain promising at the close of the sixties, while the CPC had never seemed able to attract more than a small handful of adherents from the subcontinent. Because the Vietnam issue had grown to such overwhelming proportions, the loss of the CPC was not of critical effect, and the Russian Churches themselves had contributed so vigorously to the support of the struggle that they could hope for considerable influence in Southeast Asia as a result. Towards the end of the decade the Russian Church had devoted considerable energy to Japan, which was rapidly assuming a dominant role in the Far East, with a number of important visits, consultations, and conferences already to its credit. Hence there was a promising basis on which a growing influence might be built, and, indeed, Japan seemed to occupy an increasingly prominent position among the Church's considerations as the decade drew to a close.

There were some indications that new opportunities might unfold for the Russian Church in the Far East during the seventies. The withdrawal of American influence from Japanese Orthodoxy in connection with the Moscow Patriarchate's grant of autocephaly to the US Metropolia would serve to clear the way for the Russian Church, which was already represented in Japan through a small number of Japanese parishes under its jurisdiction, to establish influential relationships there. As early as 1969 the Moscow Patriarchate had expressed its willingness to be represented at the World Conference on Religion and Peace, and the conduct of the relatively large delegation from the USSR at the Conference (Kyoto, 1970), which included a large representation from the non-Christian religions of South and Southeast Asia, seemed eminently well designed to establish and foster warm relations with the other delegates. In 1968 observers from the Buddhist communities in the USSR and Ceylon were invited to attend the CPC's All Christian Peace Assembly, representing something of a departure in the CPC's approach. Finally, the fact that the Moscow Patriarchate was careful to invite representatives of non-Christian religions, including Islam and Buddhism, to the Zagorsk peace conference in 1969 would allow the utilization of that experience in exploring an All Religions approach to organized peace activities in place of the former All Christian approach of the CPC, should efforts in that direction seem desirable.

From the point of view of Soviet foreign policy, an increase in efforts in the Far East, perhaps even to the point of forming some structured attempt to capitalize upon peace sentiments among the major religions of Asia, would not be unreasonable. Numerous considerations might support such a shift in geographical emphasis at the beginning of the new decade.

In view of the reversal of fortunes the US experienced in the Vietnam War, and in view of the strength of sentiment within the US against further adventures of that sort, it would seem reasonable to suppose that for a certain period the US is not likely to react with unreasoned aggressiveness to Soviet manœuvres. Hence it would seem safe to contemplate a reduction in the intensity of the East-West confrontation, at least for the short term, allowing a somewhat greater allocation of resources to another theatre, in this case the Far East.

Secondly, the Sino-Soviet dispute has attained perilous dimensions, and war has become a genuine possibility. This is not to imply, of course, that as yet the USSR expects or wants war with China, preemptive or otherwise; but no great degree of perspicacity is required to recognize that such a war may come, regardless of efforts to avert it. In such circumstances, it is only reasonable to take whatever advance precautions seem feasible against the contingency of war in the Far East.

In this regard, the Church could be of some service to the USSR. It will be recalled that Soviet foreign policy was exceedingly fortunate in having well-organized, functioning facilities for peace propaganda in being before the outbreak of the two previous major wars: the World Peace Council in the case of the Korean War, and the Prague Christian Peace Conference in the case of the Vietnam War. Through these agencies, the Churches were able to render significant services in support of Soviet interests in those conflicts. In present conditions, when inter-religious dialogue and co-operation are very much in vogue, the Church could certainly hope to find points of common interest with the religions of the Far East, particularly among those which incline towards pacifism, such as Buddhism. In case of war, considerable benefits might be achieved in reducing Soviet problems on the periphery of the conflict and, in particular, in inhibiting the development of alliances with China.

Hence there are considerations which would indicate that a shift of Church interests towards the Far Eastern theatre would not be an unreasonable prospect. It should be noted, however, that the Church's activities in the Far East were still very much in a developmental state at the close of the sixties, and no firm trends had yet crystallized. The area is of definite concern for Soviet foreign policy. How, or whether, the Church will attempt to increase the services it can render there remains to be seen as the developing interests of the seventies take shape.

11 Limitations and Opportunities

THERE are general considerations which set the limits and define the opportunities for the Soviet State in maintaining a religious dimension in its foreign policy operations. The dynamics of Church co-operation with the international interests of the State allow for great flexibility and a broad range of possible approaches and endeavours, but by no means does the State enjoy unlimited scope in its utilization of the Churches in international affairs, for to exceed the limits inherent in the situation, and to ignore the existing opportunities, would necessarily destroy any genuine prospects for success in the endeavour.

Even when the country's Churches themselves are willing to co-operate with the goals of Soviet foreign policy without reservation, as might seem to be the case, for example, with the Russian Orthodox and Russian Baptist Churches, there are definite limitations inherent in State use of the services offered by the Churches.

Perhaps the most basic of such limitations is the unavoidable conflict between the State's foreign aspirations, which are committed to the extension of Soviet influence in the modern world, and its domestic goals, which are to effect the eventual, total disappearance of religion from society. In order to retain their credibility in foreign relations, the Churches must be allowed to retain a certain base domestically, for otherwise, if churchmen in international affairs are leaders of non-existent Churches at home (as is largely the case with Soviet Buddhism), eventually the contradiction will become transparent and such leaders will be as ineffectual as the Exarchates of the Moscow Patriarchate in East Germany or New York. Hence the exploitation of the Churches in foreign policy is limited by the domestic religious policy; and to some degree the converse is also true.

When the State attempts to further both of these contradictory goals simultaneously, eventually it may expect a loss of credibility in its international efforts. In the sixties the State instituted a vastly expanded use of the services of the Church in international life, while concurrently engaging in a serious effort to reduce the influence of religion at home. In such conditions, regardless of how skilfully State and Church alike attempt to conceal the domestic situation from the outside world, in the long run the contradiction is certain to be discovered, with a corresponding loss of credibility abroad. If for no other reason, attempts by indigenous religious dissenters, such as the *Initsiativniki*, to publicize their cause will almost inevitably cause fissures in the news blockade. Although Western awareness of the domestic situation of religion in the USSR is still sufficiently slight to allow continued credibility to the churchmen who are active in international life, the contradiction is nevertheless inherent, and the religious dimension of Soviet foreign policy must exercise some care accordingly.

Even with the most co-operative of Churches, there is always the risk that the Church at large will eventually become restive, and that the willingness of the leadership to offer full co-operation to the State despite the increasing difficulties State policies are causing domestically will eventually be repudiated by the membership of their Church. This was certainly the case with the *Initsiativniki*, who declared the denominational leaders excommunicate on these grounds. This dissatisfaction was widespread among the Baptists, for even among the non-schismatics, vigorous complaints were registered at the Baptist Congress of 1963 that the leaders were emphasizing foreign activities to the neglect of domestic needs.[1] This possibility can be averted, however, as was evident in the case of Nikolai, who, although the example *par excellence* of willingness to co-operate with the foreign activities of the State, nevertheless was deeply respected as a pastor within his Church; his death in 1961 occasioned immense, genuine, and universal sorrow throughout the Russian Church. But in every case, there is always a risk that power abroad may not be accompanied by similar acceptance at home, and thus the services which a cleric can render may eventually be limited by the erosion of his domestic base of power. In the case of Nikodim, for example, it is not yet clear how successfully his acceptability within the Church in Russia has been maintained, and the possibility of domestic protests against his leadership undermining his credibility in the West has not yet been demonstrably precluded.[2]

A further limitation experienced even with the most co-operative of churchmen is the range of topics which they can handle effectively. As the experience with the peace propaganda of the Stalin period demonstrated, certain approaches simply are not believable, and the questions raised by the American delegation to Russia in 1956 demonstrated how small is the receptivity for this sort of activity. Again, the Patriarch's position on the Prague invasion came perilously close to the limit of credibility. Hence the use of religion in Soviet foreign policy can promise success only on a limited range of topics and approaches, and by no means can the Churches be effectively used in indiscriminate support of every activity undertaken by the State.

Finally, use of the services of the Church in Soviet foreign policy entails certain possibilities for contra-productive results. Successful operations, while rendering immediate service to the foreign policy needs of the moment, can by their very success limit the range of Soviet foreign policy in making further use of the Church. A case in point would be the experience in the WCC, where the Russian Church has built a sufficiently strong base of acceptance as to render it all but impossible for this field of activity to be terminated without entailing massive losses of prestige and effectiveness in all other areas of Church endeavour.

Perhaps even more important for the State is the possibility that the Church, even while rendering service to the needs of Soviet foreign policy, may concurrently be able to achieve benefits for its own interests. The increasing skills acquired by contact with Western theological and social approaches, or the growth of public support for the Russian Church in Western public opinion, or other, similar advantages which may accrue, could, from the viewpoint of the USSR's domestic struggle to reduce the Church's influence in society, be of sufficient magnitude in increasing the Church's ability to meet atheism's challenge as to render questionable the entire subject of the use of religion in international activity. Benefits gained abroad might become too small to counterbalance domestic difficulties. It should be noted, however, that this remains a somewhat remote possibility, for at least during the sixties the services rendered by the Church abroad entailed few, if any, visible contra-productive effects at home, and the USSR seemed fully able to enjoy the benefits of the Church's services in Soviet foreign policy while simultaneously restricting its activities inside the USSR within exceedingly narrow limits.

Thus even when the Churches are willing to offer unreserved co-operation, Soviet foreign policy encounters limits in using their services. Where the Churches refuse to co-operate, however, the limits have so far proved insuperable, and it simply is not possible to derive any significant benefits from them in foreign affairs. In numerous cases in Eastern Europe it has been demonstrated that Churches which refuse to co-operate cannot be made to conform to Soviet desires in foreign relations; where force has been applied consistently and without respite, Churches have been destroyed entirely, as in the case of Catholicism in Russia, or have gone underground, as in the case of Jehovah's Witnesses throughout Eastern Europe and the USSR, without offering to co-operate, and hence these unco-operative Churches are quite useless from the point of view of Soviet foreign policy. Nor have attempts to create competing infra-structures to serve the needs of the State in foreign affairs been at all successful. Such organizations as ' Pax ' in Poland, or the ' Peace Movement of Catholic Clergy ' in Czechoslovakia, simply had no credibility at all in foreign affairs, and hence were totally unable to overcome the disability of the dominant Church's refusal to co-operate.

In Eastern Europe, and perhaps to a smaller degree in the USSR as well, nationalism remains a factor which can pose great problems in the utilization of religion in foreign policy. Churches whose co-operation with the State is motivated, at least in part, by an identification with the nation and its history seem prone to follow the dictates of nationalism, rather than of Soviet leadership. In the USSR the nationalistic background of Russian Orthodoxy's co-operation with the State provides it with an important means of access to the Russian people, and any promotion of the Church for foreign consumption risks a similar promotion of its status among the Russian people. Similarly, Muslims are prone to emphasize their nationalistic background in their foreign activities. In Eastern Europe the Churches of Bulgaria, Rumania, Yugoslavia, the German Democratic Republic, and elsewhere are deeply nationalistic. Where the national interests come into conflict with those of the USSR, these churches, so far from being loyal to Soviet foreign policy, tend to serve the national interest, as the protests against the Prague invasion by the Rumanian and Serbian Orthodox Churches illustrate.

The proclamation of the autonomy of the Macedonian Orthodox Church in Yugoslavia in 1967 provides a vivid example of the problem of nationalism in religious foreign affairs. A product of Yugoslavia's movement towards greater national autonomy within the federative structure, the creation of the Macedonian Church complicated the international confusion in the Balkans by increasing the religious expression of the nationalism rampant in the area. The rest of Orthodoxy was persuaded to follow the Serbian Patriarchate's lead in refusing to recognize the new Church, which had unilaterally renounced its former status as a component of the Serbian Church. Church and State alike in Bulgaria, where recidivist sentiments are powerful, considered the formation of the new Church a Yugoslav manœuvre to consolidate its hold on Macedonia, which many Bulgarians consider should belong by rights to Bulgaria; and Greece, which likewise cherishes claims to

Macedonia, was similarly incensed. In the Orthodox emigration, the creation of the new Church had powerful potential for reducing the Bulgarian (and hence the Soviet) influence, for prior to the creation of an independent Macedonian Church, Orthodox émigrés from Macedonia had tended to affiliate with the Bulgarian, rather than the Serbian, parishes abroad. In short, the Macedonian affair raised immense problems for the conduct of international Church affairs, and vividly illustrated the problems which can arise because of nationalism in the conduct of international religious affairs.

With regard to the Churches from the non-Soviet world, a considerable array of limitations is inherent in the implementation of a religious dimension in Soviet foreign policy. Perhaps the most insuperable is the difficult fact, which Soviet practitioners seem curiously prone to forget, that it is simply not realistic to expect indiscriminate support for every aspect of Soviet policy, no matter how aggressive it may be. The dynamics of Church-State relations in the USSR permit the State to rely on the Churches for support regardless of the action in question, as was evident in the reactions to the Prague invasion. But the reactions of foreign Churches to the same event demonstrated that Soviet foreign policy cannot hope for this sort of unlimited support from Churches which lie outside the regions of Soviet political control.

Not even the most progressive of Western churchmen, with deep and steadfast sympathies for the USSR, are free of limitations from the point of view of Soviet foreign policy. One basic problem is the lack of influence such churchmen can retain, for their credibility seems to decrease in proportion to the degree to which their activities demonstrate an uncritical bias towards Soviet political outlooks, as was illustrated in the case of the ' Red Dean ' of Canterbury. Furthermore, with the exclusion of those against whom threats can be used effectively (as, for example, some of the former members of the Nazi Party), these churchmen remain honest men, and it requires a considerable degree of attention to ensure that their loyalties to Soviet interpretations of world events will remain unwavering. Even the most willing supporters can be alienated by actions which are too obviously incompatible with the ethical norms to which these churchmen are, ultimately, loyal, as was illustrated in the alienation which developed in the CPC, and particularly in Hromadka himself, as a result of the invasion. Finally, such churchmen are accustomed to independence in their religious lives, and, while they may co-operate most harmoniously, they also have a tendency to embarrass Soviet foreign policy with ideas, suggestions, and ambitions of their own which have nothing to do whatsoever with the desires of the Soviet State. The episode of the Christian-Marxist Dialogue may provide an illustration of this annoying independence.

The root problem in dealing with the Western Churches is that however much they may be willing to consider common cause on specific issues or approaches, their basic goals are fundamentally different from those of Soviet foreign policy. Even the most radical of Churches are motivated by goals which are Christian in origin, whereas the chief goal of Soviet foreign policy is the extension of the influence of the USSR in the world (or the extension of Communism, which, in the contemporary Soviet lexicon, amounts to the same thing). For example, in the Churches the concern for social justice is immediate and genuine, rather than a tactical device to hasten the demise of an opponent's economic or political system. Revolution is to be supported in the hope of achieving justice, rather than as an opportunity for extension of Soviet power. In the last analysis it might be possible to postulate a large measure of congruency between Christian and Marxist social ideals, as the CPC theology attempted with some success; but in the practical world of Soviet foreign policy, the words and slogans have a radically different meaning, one which is, ultimately, quite incompatible with apparently similar formulations of the Churches.

Finally, the Western Churches have only a limited potential for Soviet interests because of their inflexibility. Only a certain degree of modification in the patterns of Soviet policy is possible before Western churchmen will refuse to follow the contradictory directions placed before them. Soviet foreign policy depends, at least in part, upon considerable flexibility for achieving pragmatic success, and must be able to reverse itself completely if unexpected opportunities arise. Whereas the Russian Churches pose less of a problem in this regard and can be induced to support an immense variety of Soviet activities, Western Churches are less malleable and cannot be expected to offer an inexhaustible willingness to acquiesce in complete contradictions in the conduct of Soviet foreign affairs.

The ultimate limitation inherent in a religious dimension in Soviet foreign policy is the fact that religion can provide, at best, only a marginal contribution to Soviet interests. Particularly in international politics, the world is secular, and the influence of the Churches is by no means a dominant factor in the concert of powers, alliances, parties, and concerns with which Soviet foreign policy is engaged. The course of international life does not look to the Church for guidance, and if pretensions to a rather medieval assessment of the Church's power to admonish and guide nations may occasionally appear in the overtones of proclamations from Rome or Geneva or Moscow or New York, the fact remains that however powerful the voice of the Church may be, it is but one of several competing interests which act together to determine the conduct of international political life. Even should the USSR enjoy absolute success in winning the support of the Churches, this would still represent only a fractional gain in the competition for influence in a secular world. Hence the role of religion in Soviet foreign policy is intrinsically marginal, helpful to be sure, but incapable of aspiring to more than a limited level of interest.

Despite all such inescapable limitations, a considerable range of opportunity remains to the State in utilizing a religious dimension in its foreign policy. With regard to its co-operative Churches, there are vast opportunities for eliciting further co-operation. Many of these leaders have a strong and sincere desire to serve their country. This may spring from a world view which can conceive of only a single order in human affairs, in which the Christian is theologically obliged to serve the authorities which providence has established over society. Such an outlook was postulated by the Moscow priest, V. Shpiller, in explaining the conduct of churchmen of the post-Revolutionary generation, such as Nikodim.[3] Others, such as Hromadka, while recognizing the faults of the system, may be sincerely convinced that on balance it will achieve goals (justice, equality, etc.) to which Christians also must aspire. This approach may perhaps be compared to the pretensions of an earlier American generation to a ' manifest destiny '; for a secular government is, by definition, un-Christian, just as an atheistic government is. The dominant motivation in the co-operating Churches, however, is probably an acceptance of distasteful obligations to serve the State in the area of politics in order to receive sufficient concessions in return to allow the continued functioning of the Church within society. Despite the withdrawal of many of the earlier concessions during the sixties, this rationale continues to offer the State opportunities for achieving co-operation. Once the bargain has been accepted, the Church can ill afford to renounce it, regardless of the fact that the corresponding concessions are withdrawn gradually, lest it lose all of the dwindling remainder and, in the face of the State's total (as opposed to near-total) hostility, the Church cease to exist as an institution in Soviet society.

Hence it would seem that the State continues to enjoy good prospects for continued enjoyment of the services of the co-operative Churches in the conduct of its foreign policy. A considerable fund of genuine willingness to serve remains in the Churches, and the losses suffered by the Churches in the USSR during the sixties have not yet driven them to repudiate the agreement to serve the political interests of the State in return for being allowed to function, even on an increasingly restricted scale, in society.

Soviet foreign policy has some small basis for hoping that eventually those Churches which heretofore have refused to co-operate may be brought to a position in which opportunities for enlisting their aid in some of its activities might develop. Particularly in view of the possibilities for *rapprochement* with Rome, the Catholic Churches in Poland, Czechoslovakia, and Hungary might eventually soften their adamant hostility. The negotiations with Rome for regularizing the diocesan structures in the Oder-Neisse regions of Poland have already been of some small service in supporting the long effort to establish the present structure of Eastern Europe as permanent, while the relative success of the Yugoslav government in reaching accord with Rome in matters relating to the Croatian population, and the corresponding increase in support the government receives from Croatian Catholics, serve to illustrate the transformations which might be expected from *rapprochement* with Rome.

Furthermore, the USSR may feel that time is on its side with regard to the more recalcitrant Churches. With the growing acceptance of the situation within the Soviet sphere of political hegemony, it might perhaps be hoped that the Churches which heretofore have resisted the governments imposed on their societies may strive for an improvement in conditions by seeking some more harmonious relation with the State. The chief illustration of such a process is to be found in the decision to form an independent East German Evangelical Church in 1969, abandoning the former all-German concept of the Evangelical Church of Germany.

Nevertheless, it should be noted that such possibilities as these are still rather slight, and it seems probable that Soviet foreign policy can expect few immediate opportunities among those Churches which have refused to co-operate.

Considerable opportunities remain available for achieving benefits for Soviet foreign policy among the Western Churches. The interaction of the Russian Churches with those of the West has by no means reached a plateau, but is still increasing in breadth and scope, as in the recently initiated dialogue between the Russian Orthodox Church and US

Catholics. There are no indications to suggest that the Russian Churches cannot hope to continue to expand their activities in the West, and there is every reason to expect that further increases in their impact on Western Church affairs may be achieved. Such an estimate presumes, of course, that the trend towards a neo-Stalinist approach will not be carried to extremes, for the blunt and uncompromising patterns of the international activities of the Russian Church during the Stalin era would probably result in a swift loss of effective influence in the Western Churches. There are no indications that disillusionment has yet set in, and provided the activities of the Russian churchmen in serving the interests of Soviet foreign policy can avoid alienation of the Western Churches, numerous opportunities remain available.

Of considerable importance in the assessment of opportunities for effective use of the religious dimension of Soviet foreign policy in the West is the great strength of liberal (as opposed to conservative or traditional) Christianity in Western Protestantism and, increasingly, in Catholicism. No signs have yet appeared to suggest any retreat from the liberal approach, such as occurred after World War I in Europe, and after World War II throughout the West, with the rise of Existentialism and the Neo-Orthodox movement. To the contrary, the prevailing liberal sentiments have evolved in the opposite direction, with radical positions gaining strength at an increasing rate in the latter part of the sixties. The existence of a strong current of liberal Christianity offers some opportunities for Soviet foreign policy which might not be available were a less innovative approach dominant in the West.

From its inception the Soviet State has enjoyed great success in identifying itself with progressive, liberal movements, especially in political affairs. Soviet foreign policy has been able to build on this image of the USSR as the epitome and leader of liberal causes, and in many of its activities it has elicited strong support from liberal circles throughout the world. The techniques, rationales, and vocabularies which have facilitated this liberal image for the USSR are obviously applicable in the religious sphere as well, as the increasing tendency to agree with Soviet prescriptions for the ills of the underdeveloped world illustrates.

Among the more radical elements in the West, particularly in the younger generation, this image has suffered extensive deterioration during the past decade. In view of the severity of recent domestic policies and the harshness of the insistence on conformity in Eastern Europe, the USSR is no longer considered quite so exemplary among the most radical elements in the West. The general reaction would not seem to be hostility so much as boredom; the USSR is considered a part of the Establishment, and simply is not interesting when more dynamic, romantic symbols (China, Cuba, North Vietnam) are available.

But Soviet foreign policy has not been much inconvenienced by this partial erosion of its image. The existing power structure in the West is still in the hands of a generation which was educated in the patterns of the older liberalism, whose idiom has been employed with immense success in Soviet foreign policy. Thus the congruency of symbols, stated goals, and ideals can expect to offer continued opportunity for eliciting sympathy and support for Soviet foreign policy aspirations.

The highly developed and influential stream of social concern in Western Christianity (and, perhaps to a lesser degree, in Islam) offers immense opportunities to the USSR, for, as has been noted, the goals of Marxism were drawn from the Judæo-Christian heritage, and are eminently compatible with the contemporary Christian emphasis on the social implications of the faith. Social concerns seem stronger than ever in Western Christianity, and, indeed, are never likely to disappear. Thus the ability of Soviet foreign policy to structure at least some of its activities in terms which are consonant with the social emphases of the Western Church will continue to offer numerous opportunities for eliciting sympathy and support.

Finally, emphasis on concrete social implications inevitably can lead to a degree of frustration in a world which seems reluctant to surrender cherished injustices. Continual disappointment in the search for some rapid road to justice can result in bitter impatience with the *status quo*, a desire to have done with the system itself rather than tolerate the continuation of injustice and misery. Such sentiments are open to new approaches, and, provided the USSR properly exploits its desire, alleged or real, to end injustice by application of Soviet remedies, Soviet foreign policy can expect to discover important opportunities among those impatient with the continuation of injustice in the world.

Thus it would appear that a broad field of opportunity remains for the effective employment of a religious dimension in Soviet foreign policy. The State continues to enjoy an all but unlimited willingness to serve on the part of its co-operative Churches, while even the unco-operative Churches may eventually elect to become more amenable to contributing to the over-all goals of their societies. In the world outside manifold opportunities remain, some of them yet to be explored. Particularly during the sixties the Russian Churches have been able to render useful assistance to the successful execution of Soviet foreign policy, and in the seventies continuing and expanding opportunities for such service are available in the West and throughout the Third World. It seems certain that for the foreseeable future, throughout the vast range and area of interests and activities of Soviet foreign policy, the Churches of the USSR will render service whenever they have the opportunity. As it has done for the past quarter of a century, religion will continue to play a minor, but significant and increasingly pervasive, role in Soviet foreign policy.

Notes

CHAPTER 1: INTRODUCTION

1 For examples, see pp. 8, 18, 58, 86, 133, and 138 below.
2 For detailed examination of this issue, see William C. Fletcher, *A Study in Survival: the Church in Russia, 1927–1943* (1965).
3 See William C. Fletcher, *Nikolai: Portrait of a Dilemma* (1968), pp. 67–9.
4 e.g. Matthew Spinka, in his *The Church in Soviet Russia* (1956).
5 e.g. Metropolitan Nikolai, in his *Za mir* [For peace] (1955), pp. 70–1.
6 For more detailed treatment of the following historical survey, see Fletcher, *A Study in Survival, passim.*
7 *Izvestiia*, 27 June 1923.
8 *Izvestiia*, 18 Aug. 1927.
9 William Chauncey Emhardt, *Religion in Soviet Russia* (1929), p. 156.
10 *Izvestiia*, 16 Feb. 1930.
11 Russian Orthodox Eastern Church (abbr. hereafter as ROEC), *Patriarkh Sergii i ego dukhovnoe nasledstvo* [Patriarch Sergii and his spiritual legacy] (1947), pp. 322–31.

CHAPTER 2: CONSOLIDATION OF HEGEMONY

1 For the foreign activities of the Russian Church in the immediate post-war period, see Wassilij Alexeev, *Russian Orthodox Bishops in the Soviet Union, 1941–1953* (1954, in Russian), and *The Foreign Policy of the Moscow Patriarchate, 1939–1953* (1953, in Russian); Spinka, pp. 101–47; ROEC, *Patriarkh Sergii . . . nasledstvo*, pp. 341–57; and Fletcher, *Nikolai*, pp. 54–84.
2 For the Patriarchate's report, see *Zhurnal Moskovskoi Patriarkhii* [Journal of the Moscow Patriarchate, hereafter cited as *ZhMP*], No. 5 (May) 1945.
3 ROEC, *Patriarkh Sergii . . . nasledstvo*, p. 347.
4 For a detailed, sympathetic account of the visit, see M. Kurdiumov and N. Poltoratskii, eds, *Dni primireniia: Mitropolit Nikolai v Parizhe* [Days of reconciliation: Metropolitan Nikolai in Paris] (1946).
5 For the Council of 1948, see ROEC, *Deianiia soveshcheniia glav i predstavitelei avtokefal'nykh pravoslavnykh tserkvei v sviazi s prazdno-vaniem 500 letiia avtokefalii Russkoi Pravoslavnoi Tserkvi* [Proceed-

ings of the conference of heads and representatives of the autocephalous Orthodox Churches in connection with the 500th anniversary of the autocephaly of the Russian Orthodox Church] (1949). A translation of major portions of this work was published by the YMCA Press in Paris, 1952, entitled *Major Portions of the Proceedings of the Conference of the Heads of the Autocephalous Orthodox Churches held in Moscow, July 1948.*

CHAPTER 3: THE COLD WAR

[1] For a survey of the participation of the Russian Church in the peace campaign, see William B. Stroyen, *Communist Russia and the Russian Orthodox Church, 1943–1962* (1967), pp. 54–64; Spinka, pp. 147–50; Fletcher, *Nikolai*, pp. 96–134.

[2] *ZhMP*, No. 9 (Sept.) 1949, reprinted in Nikolai, *We Will Defend Peace !* (1955), pp. 16–24.

[3] *ZhMP*, No. 7 (July) 1954, reprinted in Nikolai, *Za mir*, pp. 71–2.

[4] *ZhMP*, No. 3 (Mar.) 1951, reprinted in Nikolai, *We Will Defend Peace !*, pp. 69–75.

[5] Ibid.

[6] *ZhMP*, No. 9 (Sept.) 1949, reprinted in Nikolai, *We Will Defend Peace !*, pp. 20–1.

[7] ROEC, *Conference in Defence of Peace of All Churches and Religious Associations in the USSR* (1952), pp. 88–9.

CHAPTER 4: THE CHRISTIAN PEACE CONFERENCE

[1] Unless otherwise specified, data in this chapter are drawn from the various publications of the CPC: *Christian Peace Conference* (bimonthly, hereafter cited as *CPC*); *Information Bulletin of the Christian Peace Conference* (mimeographed, irregular); and various conference programmes, speeches, working papers, and booklets issued in Prague by the CPC, such as *Task and Witness* (1958), *My Covenant Is Life and Peace* (1964), and *Seek Peace and Pursue It* (1968).

[2] *Cheŝky Bratr* [Bohemian Brother], Mar. 1964.

[3] *CPC*, Nov. 1962, p. 15.

[4] Ibid. Nov. 1963, p. 166.

[5] Ibid. Mar. 1963, p. 69.

[6] Ibid. Mar. 1964, p. 185.

[7] Ibid. Jan. 1963, p. 44.

⁸ Ibid. Mar. 1963, p. 60.

⁹ Ibid. p. 50.

¹⁰ Hromadka's theology receives extensive treatment in Charles C. West, *Communism and the Theologians : Study of an Encounter* (1958), and also in West's ' Josef Hromadka ', in Thomas E. Bird, ed., *Modern Theologians : Christian and Jewish* (1966).

¹¹ *CPC*, Mar. 1963, p. 59.

¹² The following analysis is based on the ' Statute of the Christian Peace Conference ', in *My Covenant Is Life and Peace,* pp. 20–2.

¹³ *Seek Peace and Pursue It*, p. 22.

¹⁴ cf. *Kostnické Jiskry* [Sparks from Constance], 14 Aug. 1968, translated in *Religion in Communist Dominated Areas* (hereafter cited as *RCDA*), 15/30 Sept. 1968, p. 154.

¹⁵ Ibid. pp. 148–9.

¹⁶ *ZhMP*, No. 10 (Oct.) 1968, pp. 2–3.

¹⁷ A report on the conference may be found in *ZhMP*, No. 9 (Sept.) 1968, pp. 46–59.

¹⁸ *Information Bulletin of the CPC*, Dec. 1969.

CHAPTER 5: THE THIRD WORLD

¹ e.g. *ZhMP*, No. 7 (July) 1965, pp. 14–26; No. 2 (Feb.) 1967, pp. 17–20; No. 2 (Feb.) 1968, pp. 50–4; *Izvestiia*, 1 Jan. 1969.

² *RCDA*, 15/31 Aug. 1966, p. 130.

³ *Kostnické Jiskry*, 6 Sept. 1967.

⁴ *Ecumenical Press Service* (hereafter cited as *EPS*), 27 July 1967, p. 4.

⁵ *Kostnické Jiskry*, 6 Sept. 1967.

⁶ *Information Bulletin of the CPC*, Dec. 1964.

⁷ *ZhMP*, No. 5 (May) 1968, p. 34.

⁸ Ibid. No. 12 (Dec.) 1969, pp. 17–20.

⁹ e.g. *RCDA*, 15 May 1967, pp. 76–7.

¹⁰ Ibid. 31 Oct. 1964, pp. 143–4.

¹¹ e.g. *ZhMP*, No. 6 (June) 1967, pp. 54–8; *Kostnické Jiskry*, 1 Mar. 1967, translated in *RCDA*, 30 Apr. 1967, pp. 65–9.

¹² *ZhMP*, No. 1 (Jan.) 1967, pp. 32–6.

¹³ cf. ibid. No. 7 (July) 1967, pp. 17–18.

¹⁴ Ibid. No. 9 (Sept.) 1966, pp. 34–6; No. 4 (Apr.) 1966, pp. 35–6.

¹⁵ M. P. Mchedlov, ' Leninskii printsip edinstva marksistov i veruiushchikh trudiashchikhsia v bor'be za sotsial'nyi progress ' [The Leninist principle of the unity of Marxists and believing workers in the struggle for social progress], in Academy of Sciences of the USSR, *Voprosy nauchnogo ateizma* [Problems of scientific atheism], viii (1969), 345–6.

[16] Ibid. p. 344; cf. I. P. Grigulevich, ' Novoe i staroe v latinoamerikanskom katolitsizme ' [The new and the old in Latin American Catholicism], ibid. vi (1968), 367–72.

[17] Ibid. pp. 358–9.

[18] *ZhMP*, No. 12 (Dec.) 1967, pp. 42–7.

[19] *ZhMP*, No. 11 (Nov.) 1967, pp. 56–7; *Katolické Noviny*, 30 Oct. 1966; *Kostnické Jiskry*, 22 Mar. 1967.

[20] See below, p. 75.

[21] e.g. *Azia i Afrika Segodnia* [Asia and Africa today], No. 6 (June) 1945.

[22] S. Arutiunov and G. Svetlov, ' Novye bogi Iaponii ' [New gods of Japan], *Nauka i Religiia*, No. 11 (Nov.) 1968, pp. 51–5.

[23] e.g. *EPS*, 27 Nov. 1969, p. 13.

[24] See pp. 115–16 below.

[25] *ZhMP*, No. 7 (July) 1970, pp. 2–4.

[26] *ZhMP*, No. 12 (Dec.) 1960, p. 6.

[27] *EPS*, 16 June 1966, p. 12.

[28] Ibid. 14 May 1964, p. 6.

[29] *ZhMP*, No. 1 (Jan.) 1967, pp. 55–60.

[30] *Neue Zeit*, 10 June 1967.

[31] *ZhMP*, No. 4 (Apr.) 1968, p. 4, and No. 5 (May), 1968, pp. 6–7.

CHAPTER 6: ISLAM AND BUDDHISM

[1] G. Z. Sorkin, *Pervyi s"ezd narodov vostoka* [The first congress of the peoples of the East] (1961), pp. 8–9.

[2] Walter Z. Laqueur, *The Soviet Union and the Middle East* (1959), p. 23.

[3] Sorkin, *passim*.

[4] Walter Kolarz, *Religion in the Soviet Union* (1961), p. 410.

[5] Laqueur, pp. 36–7; Bhabani Sen Gupta, *The Fulcrum of Asia* (1970), p. 52.

[6] Laqueur, pp. 29–30.

[7] Kolarz, pp. 426–8; Robert Conquest, *Religion in the USSR* (1968), p. 74.

[8] *Bol'shaia sovetskaia entsiklopediia* [Large Soviet encyclopedia], xviii. 518–19.

[9] Quoted in Conquest, p. 75.

[10] S. Dorzhenov, ' Musul'manin li ia? ' [Am I a Muslim?], *Nauka i Religiia*, No. 4 (Apr.) 1967, p. 52.

[11] Kolarz, p. 432.

[12] Conquest, p. 67.

[13] Georg von Stackelberg, ' The Tenacity of Islam in Soviet Central Asia ', in William C. Fletcher and Anthony J. Strover, eds, *Religion and the Search for New Ideals in the USSR* (1967), pp. 94–5.

14 Laqueur, pp. 142–3.
15 *Pravda Vostoka*, 1 Nov. 1962.
16 Laqueur, pp. 198–9.
17 Ibid. pp. 178–9; Geoffrey Wheeler, 'National and Religious Consciousness in Soviet Islam', in Max Hayward and William C. Fletcher, eds, *Religion and the Soviet State : a Dilemma of Power* (1969), pp. 194–5.
18 e.g. T. Rakhimov, 'Velikoderzhavnaia politika Mao Tsze-duna i ego gruppy v natsional'nom voprose' [The great-power policy of Mao Tse-tung and his group in the nationality question], *Kommunist*, No. 7 (May) 1967, pp. 116–18; *RCDA*, 31 Mar. 1967, pp. 54–5.
19 *RCDA*, 31 Mar. 1967, p. 55; 15 Apr. 1967, pp. 62–3.
20 Ibid. 15 Feb. 1966, p. 27.
21 Ibid. 30 June 1964, pp. 94–5.
22 *Pravda Vostoka*, 5 Sept. 1956.
23 *RCDA*, 4 Nov. 1963, p. 227.
24 See the reports in *Izvestiia*, 21–27 Aug. 1967.
25 Dorzhenov, 'Musul'manin li ia? ', *Nauka i Religiia*, No. 4 (Apr.) 1967, p. 52.
26 V. Morov, 'Britain: Middle Eastern Policy', *New Times*, No. 22 (31 May) 1966, p. 19.
27 I. Beliaev, 'Islamic Alliance—Who Wants It and Why', *New Times*, No. 15 (13 Apr.) 1966, pp. 12–13.
28 Laqueur, pp. 179, 236.
29 *Pravda*, 5 May 1958.
30 *Izvestiia*, 4 Nov. 1966.
31 Ibid. 16 Sept. 1970.
32 Wynfred Joshua, *Soviet Penetration into the Middle East* (1970), p. 42.
33 Ibid. pp. 42–3.
34 Kolarz, p. 429.
35 Z. A. Samad, 'Edinym frontom' [With a united front], *Nauka i Religiia*, No. 7 (July) 1969, p. 34.
36 Kolarz, p. 429.
37 Quoted in Conquest, pp. 75–6.
38 Kolarz, p. 430.
39 Ibid. p. 444.
40 *Pravda* and *Izvestiia*, 6 June 1964.
41 *Sel'skaia Zhizn'*, Apr. 1966.
42 Kolarz, p. 431.
43 Conquest, pp. 74–5.
44 Ibid. p. 77.
45 Kolarz, pp. 430–1.
46 *Pravda Vostoka*, 1 Nov. 1962.
47 M. Andreev, 'Islam za rubezhom' [Islam abroad], *Nauka i Religiia*, No. 10 (Oct.) 1965, p. 29.

[48] Ibid.
[49] Ibid. p. 30.
[50] *Izvestiia*, 23 Oct. 1970.
[51] e.g. G. Saraikin, ' " Chernye musul'mane "—kto oni? ' [The Black Muslims—who are they?], *Nauka i Religiia*, No. 4 (Apr.) 1967, pp. 59–63; L. Mitrokhin, ' " Chernye musul'mane " v SShA ' [The Black Muslims in the USA], ibid. No. 11 (Nov.) 1968, pp. 74–9.
[52] Kolarz, pp. 460–1.
[53] Ibid. p. 454.
[54] Ibid. p. 468.
[55] C. R. Bawden, ' Commentary on an Interview [Holmes Welch's] with the Hambo Lama ', *Royal Central Asian Journal*, XLIX/2 (Apr.) 1962, p. 180.
[56] *RCDA*, 31 Aug. 1964, p. 109.
[57] *World Fellowship of Buddhists News Bulletin* (hereafter cited as *WFB Bulletin*), VI/1 (Jan.–Feb.) 1969, pp. 28–9.
[58] *Report of the 9th General Conference of the World Fellowship of Buddhists* (n.d. [1969]), p. 63.
[59] Russell Webb, ' Buddhism in Hungary ', *WFB Bulletin*, VII/1 (Jan.–Feb.) 1970, pp. 3–4.
[60] *Report . . . Buddhists*, p. 1.
[61] cf. *WFB Bulletin*, VI/1 (Jan.–Feb.) 1969, p. 42.
[62] A. N. Kochetov, ' Izuchenie buddizma v SSSR ' [The study of Buddhism in the USSR], in Academy of Sciences of the USSR, *Voprosy nauchnogo ateizma*, iv (1967), 435.
[63] ROEC, *Conference in Defence of Peace of All Churches and Religious Associations in the USSR* (n.d. [1952]), pp. 216–17.
[64] *Izvestiia*, 23 and 25 Oct., 3 Nov. 1955.
[65] Quoted in G. P. Charles, ' Revival of Religion in Burma ', in id. ed., *Buddhism in Burma* (n.d. [1955?]), pp. 16–17.
[66] Kolarz, p. 460.
[67] Holmes Welch, ' An interview with the Hambo Lama ', *Royal Central Asian Journal*, XLIX/2 (Apr.) 1962, p. 172.
[68] *Report . . . Buddhists*, pp. 4, 33, 37, 42, 49.
[69] Ibid. p. 70.
[70] *Ceylon Daily News*, 12 Dec. 1969.
[71] Ibid. 2 Jan. 1970.
[72] *WFB Bulletin*, VII/4 (July–Aug.) 1970, pp. A–C.
[73] Ibid. pp. A–B.
[74] *Meeting of Asian Buddhists, Ulan-Bator, Mongolia, 1970* (n.d. [1970]), pp. 5–8. I have corrected typographical and spelling errors in the text, and eliminated some grammatical infelicities.
[75] Ibid. pp. 17–21. Corrected, as stated above.
[76] Ibid. pp. 34–43.   [77] Ibid. p. 34.

CHAPTER 7: THE EAST-WEST CONFRONTATION

[1] Arnold T. Ohrn, ed., *The Eighth Baptist World Congress* (1950), pp. 109–10.
[2] Steve Durasoff, *The Russian Protestants: Evangelicals in the Soviet Union, 1944–1964* (1969), p. 248.
[3] *EPS*, 12 Jan. 1963, p. 3.
[4] See Michael Bourdeaux, *Religious Ferment in Russia* (1968).
[5] *Spravochnik propagandista i agitatora* [Reference book of the propagandist and agitator] (1966), pp. 149–50.
[6] Comité d'Information sur la Situation des Chrétiens en Union Soviétique, *Situation des Chrétiens en Union Soviétique* (1964).
[7] *L'Humanité*, 14 Mar. 1964.
[8] *Spravochnik propagandista i agitatora*, pp. 149–50; F. Fedorenko, *Sekty, ikh vera i dela* [The sects, their faith and works] (1965), p. 166; cf. *Bratskii Vestnik* [Fraternal Herald], No. 6 (1966), p. 17.
[9] *EPS*, 25 Jan. 1968, p. 5.
[10] Michael Bourdeaux, *Patriarch and Prophets* (1970).
[11] *RCDA*, 15/31 Aug. 1966, pp. 126–8.
[12] *ZhMP*, No. 11 (Nov.) 1967, p. 13.
[13] Ibid. No. 3 (Mar.) 1968, p. 48.
[14] Ibid. No. 1 (Jan.) 1968, p. 11.
[15] e.g. *EPS*, 16 Mar. 1967, p. 5; *ZhMP*, No. 11 (Nov.) 1969, pp. 47–56.
[16] Reprinted in *ZhMP*, No. 11 (Nov.) 1962, p. 5.
[17] *EPS*, 4 May 1962, p. 10.
[18] Fletcher, *Nikolai*, pp. 67–9.

CHAPTER 8: ROME AND THE ORTHODOX WORLD

[1] See Francis McCullagh, *The Bolshevik Persecution of Christianity* (1924).
[2] e.g. Fletcher, *A Study in Survival*, pp. 48–56.
[3] e.g. *New York Times*, 19 May 1944 and 22 Mar. 1945; *Time*, 19 Mar. 1945; *Newsweek*, 2 Apr. 1945.
[4] *America*, 7 Oct. 1961, p. 3.
[5] *ZhMP*, No. 11 (Nov.) 1962, p. 13.
[6] *EPS*, 12 Oct. 1962, p. 10.
[7] *ZhMP*, No. 11 (Nov.) 1962, p. 30.
[8] *The Times*, 12 Feb. 1963.
[9] See A. Adzhubei's report on the visit, *RCDA*, 4 Nov. 1963, pp. 217–18.
[10] *ZhMP*, No. 1 (Jan.) 1965, pp. 8–9.
[11] *EPS*, 11 Feb. 1965, p. 9.   [12] Ibid. 30 Jan. 1964, p. 2.

[13] Ibid. 6 Jan. 1966, pp. 12–13.

[14] Ibid. 2 Feb. 1967, p. 9.

[15] Ibid. 14 Dec. 1967, p. 3, and 21 Dec. 1967, p. 10.

[16] *ZhMP*, No. 12 (Dec.) 1969, p. 3.

[17] Ibid.

[18] e.g. ibid. No. 6 (June) 1967, pp. 3–4.

[19] Ibid. No. 7 (July) 1968, pp. 7–8.

[20] *Guardian*, 3 Jan. 1966.

[21] *ZhMP*, No. 8 (Aug.) 1967, p. 7, and No. 9 (Sept.) 1967, pp. 2–3.

[22] *EPS*, 22 Nov. 1963, pp. 1–2.

[23] cf. ibid. 3 Aug. 1967, p. 10.

[24] Ibid. 5 Mar. 1964, p. 17.

[25] Ibid. 25 May 1967, p. 11.

[26] *ZhMP*, No. 3 (Mar.) 1968, p. 1.

[27] Ibid. pp. 1–2.

[28] *EPS*, 8 May 1969, p. 7.

[29] *New York Times*, 10 and 21 June 1966; *EPS*, 16 June 1966, p. 8.

[30] Ibid. p. 12.

[31] *New York Times*, 20 Feb. 1970.

[32] *EPS*, 4 May 1967, p. 4.

[33] *ZhMP*, No. 5 (May) 1970, pp. 6–24; No. 6 (June) 1970, pp. 69–79.

CHAPTER 9: THE WORLD COUNCIL OF CHURCHES

[1] ROEC, *Major Portions of the Proceedings of the Conference . . . July 1948*, p. 180.

[2] Fletcher, *Nikolai*, pp. 163–9.

[3] *New York Times*, 3 June 1956.

[4] Ibid. 24 Aug. 1959.

[5] 'World Conference on Church and Society', Press Release No. 33, 22 July 1966.

[6] *ZhMP*, No. 4 (Apr.) 1968, p. 34.

[7] Ibid. No. 11 (Nov.) 1967, p. 68.

[8] *EPS*, 14 Mar. 1968, p. 13.

[9] Ibid. 9 Jan. 1969, p. 11.

[10] *ZhMP*, No. 5 (May) 1967, pp. 8–9.

[11] Stroyen, p. 80.

[12] N. I. Yudin, *Pravda o Petersburgskikh 'Sviatyniakh'* [The truth about the 'shrines' of St Petersburg] (1962), translated in *RCDA*, 24 June 1963, p. 117. Cf. the testimony of Paul B. Anderson on 29 Jan. 1964, USA House of Representatives, Cttee on For. Aff., Subcttee on Europe, *Recent Developments in the Soviet Bloc*, Pt 1, Hearings, 88th Cong., 2nd sess. (Washington, DC, 1964), p. 99.

13 *Spravochnik propagandista i agitatora*, pp. 149–50.
14 *EPS*, 9 Nov. 1967, p. 7.
15 Ibid. 22 Feb. 1968, p. 2.
16 *Izvestiia*, 31 Aug. 1966, translated in Bourdeaux, *Religious Ferment in Russia*, p. 163.
17 *EPS*, 13 Feb. 1964, p. 10.
18 Ibid. 6 Feb. 1969, p. 3.
19 Ibid. 26 Oct. 1962, p. 2.
20 Ibid. 2 Nov. 1962, p. 2.
21 *ZhMP*, No. 11 (Nov.) 1962, p. 7.
22 e.g. *EPS*, 8 June 1967.
23 Ibid. 31 Aug. 1967, pp. 4–5.
24 Ibid. 16 Jan. 1969, p. 10.
25 A detailed summary of the decisions and events concerning WCC aid to the racially oppressed may be found in *EPS*, Oct. 1970, pp. 3–5. Unless otherwise indicated, the data and quotations in the treatment which follows may be found in this source.
26 *EPS*, 6 Feb. 1964, p. 10.
27 Ibid. 23 Apr. 1964, pp. 1–3.
28 Ibid. 22 Feb. 1968, p. 2.
29 Ibid. 14 Mar. 1968, p. 11.
30 Ibid. 8 June 1967, p. 2.
31 Ibid. 22 June 1967, p. 2.
32 Ibid. 17 Aug. 1967, p. 11.
33 Ibid. 31 Aug. 1967, pp. 2–3.
34 Ibid. 6 July 1967, p. 7.
35 *ZhMP*, No. 11 (Nov.) 1967, p. 70.
36 *EPS*, 22 Aug. 1968, p. 12.
37 Ibid. 29 Aug. 1968, pp. 2–3.
38 *ZhMP*, No. 10 (Oct.) 1968, pp. 1–2.

CHAPTER 11: LIMITATIONS AND OPPORTUNITIES

1 William C. Fletcher, 'Protestant Influences on the Outlook of the Soviet Citizen Today ', in id. and Anthony J. Strover, eds, *Religion and the Search for New Ideals in the USSR*, pp. 70–1.
2 cf. the appeal to the General Secretary of the WCC from Orthodox parishioners in Gorky, translated in *Eastern Churches Review*, II/4 (autumn) 1969, p. 421.
3 *Rossiia i Vselenskaia Tserkov'* [Russia and the Universal Church], No. 4, 1966, and No. 1, 1967.

Reference Bibliography

BOOKS

Alexeev, Wassilij. *The foreign policy of the Moscow Patriarchate, 1939–1953* (in Russian). New York, Research Programme on the USSR, 1953.

—— *Russian Orthodox bishops in the Soviet Union, 1941–1953* (in Russian). New York, Research Programme on the USSR, 1954.

Bol'shaia sovetskaia entsiklopediia [Large Soviet encyclopedia], xviii. Moscow, BSE Press, 1953.

Bourdeaux, Michael. *Patriarch and prophets*. London, Macmillan, 1970.

—— *Religious ferment in Russia*. London, Macmillan, 1968.

Charles, G. P. 'Revival of religion in Burma', in id. ed., *Buddhism in Burma*. Rangoon, Commission on Buddhism of the Burma Christian Council, n.d. [1955?].

Comité d'Information sur la situation des Chrétiens en Union Soviétique. *Situation des Chrétiens en Union Soviétique*. Paris, Comité d'Information . . . 1964.

Conquest, Robert. *Religion in the USSR*. London, Bodley Head, 1968.

Durasoff, Steve. *The Russian Protestants: evangelicals in the Soviet Union, 1944–1964*. Teaneck, NJ, Farleigh Dickinson Univ. Press, 1969.

Emhardt, William Chauncey. *Religion in Soviet Russia*. New York, Morehouse, 1929.

Fedorenko, F. *Sekty, ikh vera i dela* [The sects, their faith and works]. Moscow, Publishing House for Political Literature, 1965.

Fletcher, William C. *Nikolai: portrait of a dilemma*. New York, Macmillan, 1968.

—— *A study in survival: the Church in Russia, 1927–1943*. New York, Macmillan, 1965.

—— 'Protestant influences on the outlook of the Soviet citizen today', in id. and Anthony J. Strover, eds, *Religion and the search for new ideals in the USSR*. New York, Praeger, 1967.

Grigulevich, I. P. 'Novoe i staroe v latinoamerikanskom katolitsizme' [The new and old in Latin American Catholicism], in Academy of Sciences of the USSR, *Voprosy nauchnogo ateizma* [Problems of scientific atheism], vi. Moscow, Mysl', 1968.

Gupta, Bhabani Sen. *The fulcrum of Asia*. New York, Pegasus, 1970.

Joshua, Wynfred. *Soviet penetration into the Middle East*. New York, National Strategy Information Center, 1970.

Kochetov, A. N. 'Izuchenie buddizma v SSSR' [The study of Buddhism in the USSR], in Academy of Sciences of the USSR, *Voprosy nauchnogo ateizma*, iv. Moscow, Mysl', 1967.

Kolarz, Walter. *Religion in the Soviet Union*. London, Macmillan, 1961.

Kurdiumov, M. and N. Poltoratskii, eds. *Dni primireniia: Mitropolit Nikolai v Parizhe* [Days of reconciliation: Metropolitan Nikolai in Paris]. Paris, Union of Soviet Patriots Press, 1946.

Laqueur, Walter Z. *The Soviet Union and the Middle East*. London, Routledge & Kegan Paul, 1959.

McCullagh, Francis. *The Bolshevik persecution of Christianity*. New York, Dutton, 1924.

Mchedlov, M. P. 'Leninskii printsip edinstva marksistov i veruiushchikh trudiashchikhsia v bor'be za sotsial'nyi progress' [The Leninist principle of the unity of Marxists and believing workers in the struggle for social progress], in Academy of Sciences of the USSR, *Voprosy nauchnogo ateizma*, viii. Moscow, Mysl', 1969.

Meeting of Asian Buddhists, Ulan-Bator, Mongolia, 1970. N.p., n.p., n.d. [Ulan Bator, 1970].

My covenant is life and peace. Prague, Christian Peace Conference, 1964.

Nikolai, Metropolitan. *We will defend peace!* Moscow, The Patriarchate, 1955.

—— *Za mir* [For peace]. Moscow, The Patriarchate, 1955.

Ohrn, Arnold T., ed. *The eighth Baptist world congress*. Philadelphia, Pa, Judson, 1950.

Report on the 9th general conference of the World Fellowship of Buddhists. Bangkok, WFB Secretariat, n.d. [1969].

Russian Orthodox Eastern Church. *Conference in Defence of Peace of All Churches and Religious Associations in the USSR*. Moscow, The Patriarchate, n.d. [1952].

—— *Deianiia soveshcheniia glav i predstavitelei avtokefal'nykh pravoslavnykh tserkvei v sviazi s prazdnovaniem 500 letiia avtokefalii Russkoi Pravoslavnoi Tserkvi* [Proceedings of the conference of heads and representatives of the autocephalous Orthodox Churches in connection with the 500th anniversary of the autocephaly of the Russian Orthodox Church]. Moscow, The Patriarchate, 1949.

—— *Major portions of the proceedings of the conference of the heads of the autocephalous Orthodox Churches held in Moscow, July 1948*. Paris, Y.M.C.A. Press, 1952. This is an abridged translation of *Deianiia . . . Tserkvi*.

—— *Patriarkh Sergii i ego dukhovnoe nasledstvo* [Patriarch Sergii and his spiritual legacy]. Moscow, The Patriarchate, 1947.

Seek peace and pursue it. Prague, Christian Peace Conference, 1968.

Sorkin, G. Z. *Pervyi s"ezd narodov vostoka* [The first congress of the peoples of the East]. Moscow, Publishing House for Eastern Literature, 1961.

Spinka, Matthew. *The church in Soviet Russia.* New York, OUP, 1956.

Spravochnik propagandista i agitatora [Reference book of the propagandist and agitator]. Moscow, Publishing House for Political Literature, 1966.

Stackelberg, Georg von. ' The tenacity of Islam in Soviet Central Asia ', in William C. Fletcher and Anthony J. Strover, eds, *Religion and the search for new ideals in the USSR.* New York, Praeger, 1967.

' Statute of the Christian peace conference ', in *My covenant is life and peace.* Prague, Christian Peace Conference, 1964.

Stroyen, William B. *Communist Russia and the Russian Orthodox Church, 1943–1962.* Washington, DC, Catholic Univ. of America Press, 1967.

Task and witness. Prague, Christian Peace Conference, 1958.

West, Charles C. *Communism and the theologians : study of an encounter.* London, SCM Press, 1958.

—— ' Josef Hromadka ', in Thomas E. Bird, ed., *Modern theologians : Christian and Jewish.* Notre Dame, Ind., Univ. of Notre Dame Press, 1966.

Wheeler, Geoffrey. ' National and religious consciousness in Soviet Islam ', in Max Hayward and William C. Fletcher, eds, *Religion and the Soviet state : a dilemma of power.* New York, Praeger, 1969.

Yudin, N. I. *Pravda o Petersburgskikh ' Sviatyniakh '* [The truth about the ' shrines ' of St Petersburg]. Leningrad, Lenin Press, 1962.

ARTICLES

Andreev, M. Islam za rubezhom [Islam abroad]. *Nauka i Religiia,* No. 10 (Oct.) 1965.

Arutiunov, S. and G. Svetlov. Novye bogi iaponii [New gods of Japan]. *Nauka i Religiia,* No. 11 (Nov.) 1968.

Bawden, C. R. Commentary on an interview [Holmes Welch's] with the Hambo Lama. *Royal Central Asian Journal,* XLIX/2 (Apr.) 1962.

Beliaev, I. Islamic alliance—who wants it and why. *New Times,* No. 15 (13 Apr.) 1966.

Dorzhenov, S. Musul'manin li ia? [Am I a Muslim?]. *Nauka i Religiia,* No. 4 (Apr.) 1967.

Mitrokhin, L. ' Chernye musul'mane ' v SShA [The Black Muslims in the USA]. *Nauka i Religiia,* No. 11 (Nov.) 1968.

Morov, V. Britain: Middle Eastern policy. *New Times,* No. 22 (31 May) 1966.

Rakhimov, T. Velikoderzhavnaia politika Mao Tsze-duna i ego gruppy v natsional'nom voprose [The great-power policy of Mao Tse-tung and his group in the nationality question]. *Kommunist*, No. 7 (May) 1967.

Samad, Z. A. Edinym frontom [With a united front]. *Nauka i Religiia*, No. 7 (July) 1969.

Saraikin, G. 'Chernye musul'mane'—kto oni? [The Black Muslims—who are they?]. *Nauka i Religiia*, No. 4 (Apr.) 1967.

Webb, Russell. Buddhism in Hungary. *WFB Bulletin*, VII/1 (Jan.–Feb.) 1970.

Welch, Holmes. An interview with the Hambo Lama. *Royal Central Asian Journal*, XLIX/2 (Apr.) 1962.

World Council of Churches. 'World Conference on Church and Society'. Geneva, WCC Press Release No. 33, 22 July 1966.

NEWSPAPERS AND PERIODICALS

America, New York.

Azia i Afrika Segodnia [Asia and Africa Today], Moscow

Bratskii Vestnik [Fraternal Herald], Moscow.

Ceylon Daily News, Colombo.

Chešky Bratr [Bohemian Brother], Prague.

Christian Peace Conference (CPC), Prague.

Eastern Churches Review, Oxford.

Ecumenical Press Service (EPS), Geneva.

Guardian, London.

L'Humanité, Paris.

Information Bulletin of the CPC, Prague.

Izvestiia [News], Moscow.

Katolické Noviny [Catholic News], Prague.

Kommunist, Moscow.

Kostnické Jiskry [Sparks from Constance], Prague.

Nauka i Religiia [Science and Religion], Moscow.

Neue Zeit, East Berlin.

New Times, Moscow.

New York Times

Newsweek, New York.

Pravda [Truth], Moscow.

Pravda Vostoka [Truth of the East], Alma Ata.

Religion in Communist Dominated Areas (RCDA), New York.

Rossiia i Vselenskaia Tserkov' [Russia and the Universal Church], Brussels.

Royal Central Asian Journal, London.

Sel'skaia Zhizn' [Rural Life], Moscow.
Time, New York.
The Times, London.
World Fellowship of Buddhists News Bulletin, Bangkok.
Zhurnal Moskovskoi Patriarkhii (ZhMP) [Journal of the Moscow Patriarchate], Moscow.

Index